# at home café

## great food and fun for everyone!

by
Leslie Carpenter
and
Helen DeFrance

Foreword and chapter introductions by
Carol Puckett Daily

Illustrations by
Dea Dea Baker

Photography by
Harold Head

Basil Leaf Publications

Published by Basil Leaf Publications
157 N. Maple Street, Ridgeland MS 39157

ISBN 0-9760425-0-9

Printed in China by Everbest Printing Company through Four Colour Imports, Ltd., Louisville, KY

# thank you

Our deepest appreciation goes to our families: mothers and fathers, brothers and sisters, nieces and nephews, sisters-in-law and cousins for their continued love and support in this project.

Without the inspiration and encouragement of Wyatt Waters and Robert St. John we could have never taken this leap. We thank John Langston for his wisdom in guiding us on this project, and Bill Butler and the team at Butler Books for their patience and creativity in helping us create the book we wanted to publish. Without the hand-holding and patience of René Nedelkoff, we would never have learned the tangled ropes of the publishing world.

We are eternally grateful to the entire team at The Everyday Gourmet in Jackson, Mississippi, for allowing us the opportunity to build our kids classes at their legendary cooking school and to the lively crew at the Viking Cooking School in Greenwood, Mississippi, who invited us to take our show on the road.

Kathleen Bruno, Bob Pavy, and the talented cooks at the Viking Culinary Arts Centers and Viking Home Chef stores took on the daunting task of recipe testing and magically made it happen.

Sue Neville, Cathy Miller, and Sandy Rawlins are the amazing women who invited us to bring our kids program into their schools.

We'll be forever baking cookies to thank our friends and neighbors who tested, tasted, and served as sounding boards. Harold and Amy Head are at the top of our list for making us look great with his photography and her artist's eye for make up and styling. And a special word of appreciation goes to Louisa Dixon, who encouraged us when our dream seemed elusive, and to Clare Dowe and Christina Giurantano, who assist us in our kids classes and typing of our recipes and notes.

Carol Puckett Daily, sister, friend, and mentor, helped us make our dream become a reality. We went to her with our dream, and she told us the steps we needed to take and lovingly guided us through each one.

We are forever grateful to Kreis Beall, who was one of the first to believe in our vision and invited us to create the kids cooking program at the renowned Blackberry Farm, and to Sam Beall for his continued support and belief in the program.

Most of all, we thank all of the children, past and present, who have honored us by allowing us to teach them to cook.

To the kids who inspired us:
Rob, William, Myers, Annie, Martin and Katie

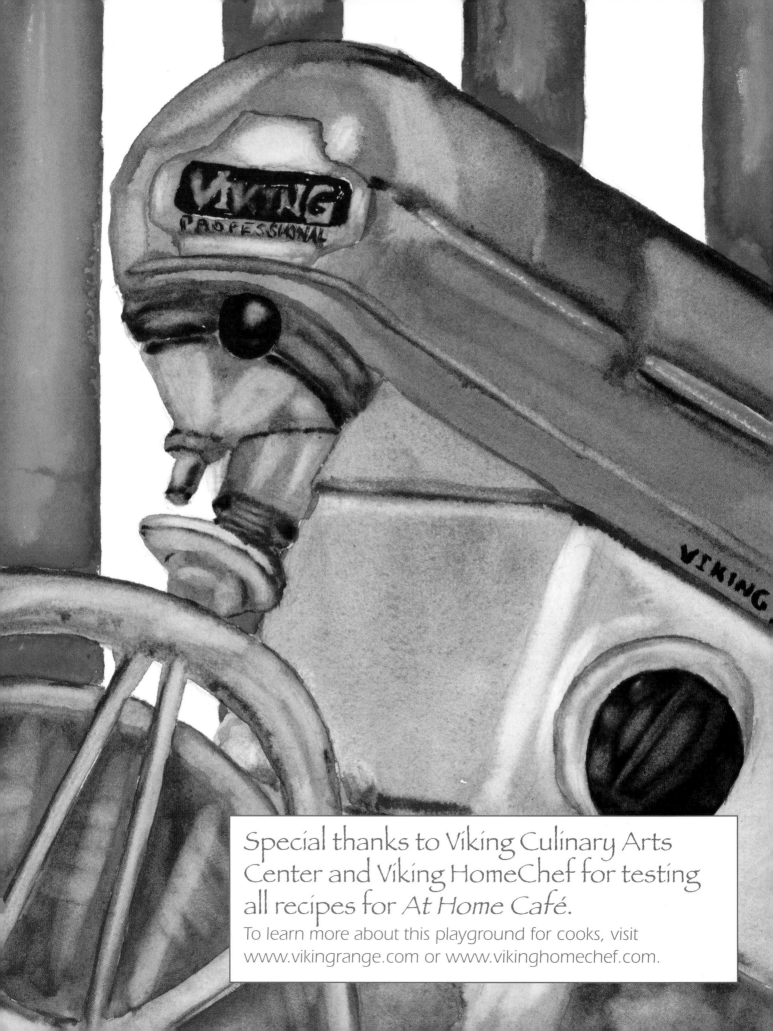

Special thanks to Viking Culinary Arts Center and Viking HomeChef for testing all recipes for *At Home Café*.

To learn more about this playground for cooks, visit www.vikingrange.com or www.vikinghomechef.com.

# table of contents

# foreword

A sister shouldn't be asked to write the foreword of a book. We know too much—and besides, being objective is totally out of the question. At Home Café, however, is a book about cooking together as a family. It's been about cooking up a book as a family as well.

Helen Puckett DeFrance is my little sister, and her business partner Leslie Andrews Carpenter might as well be a sister, too. These two women command my highest respect. They are doing something I believe is more than important. In fact it's downright laudable. They are teaching children to cook.

In a day and time when the backseat of a minivan has replaced the family table and paper bags full of fast food have replaced the dinner plate, cooking and eating with family in the home takes on a new meaning and a new importance.

Both Leslie and Helen were raised in big, noisy Southern families with mothers, grandmothers, and family cooks who presided over cheerful kitchens that were both fascinating and welcoming to children. They in turn have shared that legacy with their own children and students by saying, "Let's cook this together."

Helen and Leslie have devoted themselves as mothers and as teachers to encouraging families to cook together. They have taught hundreds of cooking classes to thousands of children and they have done so with recipes that are fun to create, delicious to eat, and always liberally seasoned with enthusiasm, patience, and love.

At Home Café is not just a cookbook for children; it is a book for families. And on the cover, between the covers, and even between the lines you'll discover that behind the two creative women who wrote this book has been an extended family. Parents, grandparents, aunts, uncles, brothers and sisters, children, nieces and nephews have shared recipes, assisted in cooking classes, swapped family stories at the dinner table, cooked together, cleaned up the kitchen, appeared in photographs, and tested recipes from Grandmother's Dinner Rolls to Mom's Marvelous Chicken Phyllo.

Cooking with Helen and Leslie is always an adventure and never a chore as you will discover in the pages of At Home Café.

Carol Puckett Daily
June 2004

# saturday morning breakfast

Saturday morning breakfast is a magical family time when we break the hurried weekday routine and the kitchen takes on a fun and more leisurely atmosphere. Children always adore squeezing oranges for their morning beverage, and it's a wonderful way to encourage them to drink fresh juice! Every young cook in our classes loves to dip a pastry brush in melted butter and "paint" sweet roll dough. Pancakes are a universal favorite and fun to make as we wait for the bubbles to rise before flipping. Leslie remembers family birthday breakfasts where she was encouraged to "eat her age" in pancakes and promises that she really did eat sixteen pancakes on her sixteenth birthday! Helen's favorite Saturday morning memory is of waking up to a mug of Kettle Tea lovingly and ceremoniously prepared by her grandfather.

Homemade Buttermilk Biscuits

Sausage Pinwheels

Sweetest Sweet Rolls

Fluffy Fluffy Pancakes

Kettle Tea

The Freshest Squeezed Orange Juice

# Homemade Buttermilk Biscuits

*4 cups all-purpose flour*
*1½ teaspoons baking powder*
*½ teaspoon baking soda*
*1 teaspoon salt*
*1 cup shortening or butter*
*2 cups buttermilk*

## Yield: about 20 biscuits

- Preheat oven to 450°.

- Place flour, baking powder, baking soda, and salt in a mixing bowl and mix thoroughly with a whisk or fork.

- Cut in shortening or butter until mixture resembles coarse crumbs.

- Add buttermilk. Stir just until the dough sticks together.

- Form dough into a ball and fold over and over on a lightly floured surface.

- Pat out dough to ½ inch thickness.

- Cut with a biscuit cutter.

- Place on an ungreased baking sheet, close together for soft-sided biscuits or 1-inch apart for crisp-sided ones.

- Bake for 5 minutes.

- Reduce oven to 400° and bake 8–10 minutes more.

## Kid Notes

» Measure dry ingredients into a bowl.

» Cut shortening into dry ingredients using a pastry blender or 2 table knives.

» Add the milk and stir only until ingredients come together.

» Be gentle when patting the dough.

## Kid Notes

» Wash your hands after crumbling the uncooked sausage on the biscuit dough.

» Lightly flour the wax paper before patting out the dough rectangle.

# Sausage Pinwheels

*1 16-ounce roll sausage (mild or hot)*
*1 recipe Homemade Buttermilk Biscuits*
   *(see page 12)*

### Yield: About 2 dozen

- Preheat oven to 400°.

- Prepare *Homemade Buttermilk Biscuits* as directed and place on a piece of lightly floured wax paper.

- Pat the dough into a 14- by 10-inch rectangle, about ¼ inch thick.

- Crumble uncooked sausage evenly over the biscuit dough.

- Beginning at the long side, roll up jellyroll style, using wax paper to help make it into a long roll.

- If not using immediately, the roll may be wrapped in foil and frozen for one month or refrigerated overnight.

- Slice roll into ½ inch pinwheels.

- Place on baking sheet, almost touching, and bake about 15–18 minutes, or until brown.

- Enjoy!

# Sweetest Sweet Rolls

### Sweet Rolls:
*1 cup whole milk*
*6 tablespoons sugar*
*1 package active dry yeast*
*3 cups plus 2 tablespoons all-purpose flour, plus more for rolling out dough*
*½ teaspoon salt*
*6 tablespoons unsalted butter, softened*
*1 egg*
*1 teaspoon vegetable oil*

### Crunchy Filling:
*¾ cup packed light brown sugar*
*1 cup crushed cornflakes*
*2 tablespoons plus 2 teaspoons ground cinnamon*
*½ teaspoon salt*
*12 tablespoons unsalted butter, melted*

### Glaze:
*2½ cups confectioners' sugar*
*4 tablespoons half and half*
*1 teaspoon vanilla extract*

Yield: 18 large rolls or 24 medium rolls

- Heat milk in a small saucepan over medium-low heat until the milk is warm. Remove from the heat.

- In a small mixing bowl combine 2 tablespoons of the sugar with the yeast and whisk in the warm milk, and let rest until slightly thickened and foamy, about 5 minutes.

- Sift the flour, the remaining 4 tablespoons of sugar, and the salt into a large mixing bowl. Add the softened butter, egg, and the yeast mixture. Stir well with a large wooden spoon until all flour is mixed in.

- Place the dough on a work surface sprinkled with 3 tablespoons of flour and knead until smooth and elastic, about 3–5 minutes. If dough is sticky, add a bit more flour and continue kneading to work it into the dough. (Alternately, mix the dough in an electric mixer fitted with a dough hook.)

- Using your hands, form the dough into a ball and lightly grease it with the vegetable oil.

- Place the dough into a large mixing bowl and cover with plastic wrap. Let rest in a warm, draft-free place and allow to rise about 1½ hours to double.

- When the dough has risen, divide it into two equal portions.

- In a small mixing bowl, make the crunchy filling by combining the brown sugar, crushed cornflakes, cinnamon, salt, and melted butter, and stirring until smooth.
- Place one portion of the dough on a lightly floured surface. Use a rolling pin that has been rubbed with flour, roll the dough into a large rectangle, about 12 inches by 9 inches.
- Using a spoon, sprinkle half of the crunchy filling over the top of the dough.
- With the long end of the rectangle facing you, roll up the dough, jellyroll style.
- Pinch the edges together and use a serrated knife to cut 1½-inch thick slices.
- Place the rounds on a large baking sheet, allowing room in between each sweet roll for the final rise.
- Repeat with the remaining dough.
- Cover sweet rolls with plastic wrap and let rest in a warm, draft-free place until risen by half their size and almost touching, about 1 hour.
- Make sure the oven rack is in the center position and preheat the oven to 350°.
- Bake until golden brown, about 30 minutes.
- Combine the glaze ingredients in a medium mixing bowl and stir until smooth.
- Remove sweet rolls from the oven and drizzle the glaze over the tops.
- Serve warm.

## Kid Notes

» Put the cornflakes in a Ziploc bag. Zip it tight and crush the cornflakes with your fingers until they look like a big bag of crumbs.

» When you see the bubbles in the yeast, you will know that it is time to mix it in the flour mixture.

» Wait for 1½ hours and see how big the dough has become! It should be doubled in size.

» Remember when using the rolling pin to dust it with flour, and roll the dough North, South, East, and West to shape it into a rectangle.

# Fluffy Fluffy Pancakes

*4 tablespoons butter, melted*
*2 cups milk*
*2 eggs, beaten*
*2 cups all purpose flour*
*½ teaspoon salt*
*2 tablespoons plus 1 teaspoon sugar*
*2 teaspoons baking powder*

## Yield: 16–18 pancakes; 6 servings

- In a large bowl, mix milk, melted butter, and egg.

- In a separate bowl, sift flour, salt, baking powder, and sugar.

- Add sifted dry ingredients to the milk, egg, and butter mixture. Whisk just until mixed.

- Ladle ¼ cup batter on lightly buttered, hot griddle or skillet.

- Cook on medium-high heat until bubbles form all over the top of the pancake.

- With a spatula, turn and cook on other side.

- Enjoy!

## Kid Notes

» Crack the eggs (see Kid Notes on page 63).

» When the pancakes are cooking, watch for bubbles in the batter. It's time to flip! Alert an adult.

» After cooking several sets of pancakes, have your adult assistant use a paper towel to wipe the skillet clean. Then melt more butter and begin again.

# Kettle Tea

*1 cup milk*
*2–3 teaspoons sugar (to your taste)*
*½ teaspoon vanilla extract*

## Yield: 1 serving

- Heat milk in a microwave-safe coffee mug for 1 minute on high in the microwave.

- Add desired amount of sugar and vanilla.

- Stir lovingly.

## Kid Notes

» This is a special good morning drink to share—it's coffee for kids!

# The Freshest Squeezed Orange Juice

*Fresh Oranges*

- Take a fresh orange, cut it in half.

- Place cut side down onto the point of the electric juicer top or hand juicer top.

- Push down on the orange half. If using an electric juicer, the juicer will activate and begin turning. If using a hand juicer, press and turn. Continue doing this until the pulp is flat against the rind and there is no more juice inside.

## Kid Notes

» You can make your very own fresh-squeezed O.J.! Once you taste it, it's hard to go back to the carton!

» An electric juicer is very inexpensive and very easy to operate!

17

# groovy groovy breakfast

We have found that breakfast is the favorite meal among young cooks. They come to our Saturday morning cooking classes in their pajamas and cook this menu. Then we all sit down to breakfast together. They love cracking eggs, using the waffle maker (supervised!), filling muffin tins, cutting fruit, playing with the biscuit dough, and getting covered in flour. Of course, canned biscuits are a fine substitute for more hurried mornings. Made with Love Blueberry Muffins were often on the breakfast table of Leslie's home as a child, where the dough was kept in the refrigerator for those special muffin mornings.

"Bomber" Biscuits

On the Go A.M. Breakfast Sandwich

Wacky Waffles

Made with Love Blueberry Muffins

"Fruitini"

# "Bomber" Biscuits

*4½ cups biscuit mix*
*8 ounces sour cream*
*1 cup club soda, divided*
*¼ cup butter, melted*

## Yield: 8 large biscuits

- Preheat oven to 450°.

- Combine sour cream with ½ cup club soda in a large bowl.

- Add 4 cups of the biscuit mix and stir with a wooden spoon until blended. Add remaining ½ cup club soda. Mix only until blended.

- On a lightly floured surface, gently pat out dough to about a 1-inch thickness.

- Use remaining ½ cup biscuit mix as needed to keep the dough from sticking.

- Cut with a large biscuit cutter. Place on baking sheet and brush with melted butter. Bake for 15 minutes at 450°.

- "Bomber" biscuits taste just like Popeye's biscuits!

## Kid Notes

» When patting out the dough, be gentle.

» Twist the biscuit cutter in the dough so that it will lift out easier.

» Handle the dough as little as possible, and you will have tender, light biscuits.

» Brush the tops of the biscuits with butter—use a pastry brush, not a paint brush!

# On the Go A.M. Breakfast Sandwich

*1 recipe "Bomber" Biscuits (see page 20), or*
*    1 10.2-ounce can refrigerated buttermilk biscuits*
*6 eggs*
*1 teaspoon salt*
*½ teaspoon pepper*
*3 tablespoons milk*
*¾ cup (about 4 ounces) cooked ham or bacon,*
*    chopped*
*1 tablespoon butter*
*½ cup cheddar cheese, shredded*

## Yield: 8 servings

- If using canned biscuits, bake as directed on can.

- Meanwhile, in a medium bowl, combine eggs, salt, pepper, and milk. Using a wire whisk, beat until foamy.

- Melt butter in a medium skillet over medium heat. Add chopped cooked ham or bacon and sauté for 2 minutes.

- Turn to low heat and pour in egg mixture; cook 4–6 minutes or until egg mixture is set, stirring and turning occasionally. Stir in cheese.

- Slice open biscuits and spoon egg mixture onto the bottom halves of the biscuits. Cover with the top halves.

- Enjoy.

## Kid Notes

» Open can of biscuits, (if using), and place them in pan.

» Crack eggs and whisk them until foamy (see Kid Notes on page 63).

» With a plastic knife or a table knife, chop the ham.

» Grate the cheese. Remember always scrape down.

# Wacky Waffles

*3 eggs*
*1 cup club soda*
*½ cup buttermilk*
*1 teaspoon baking soda*
*1¾ cups all-purpose flour*
*2 teaspoons baking powder*
*½ teaspoon salt*
*½ cup vegetable oil*
*Nonstick cooking spray*

## Yield: 8 servings

- Preheat waffle iron. Spray with nonstick cooking spray.

- In a mixing bowl, combine the ingredients and stir with a whisk until blended.

- Pour into a small pitcher or measuring cup.

- Pour batter into the waffle iron and cook until crisp and golden.

Note: Club soda makes for a light and crisp waffle.

Tip: The surface of the waffle iron becomes very hot. Be careful not to touch.

## Kid Notes

» Have fun cracking the eggs (see Kid Notes on page 63) and whisking the ingredients together.

» The batter is well blended when all of the lumps are gone.

» Be careful with the waffle iron—it gets very hot!

## Kid Notes

» Place the blueberries in a colander and put in the kitchen sink. Rinse under the faucet.

» You can pick your own blueberries or buy them. (Try not to eat them all first!)

» Make sure all of the dry ingredients make it through the sifter.

» Crack the eggs (see Kid Notes on page 63).

» You can help by greasing the muffin tins or putting paper liners in them.

# Made with Love Blueberry Muffins

⅔ cup shortening
1 cup sugar
3 eggs
3 cups flour
2½ teaspoons baking powder
1 teaspoon salt
1 cup milk
2 cups blueberries

**Yield: 16–18 muffins**

- Preheat oven to 375°.
- Grease muffin tins or line with muffin cup liners.
- Cream sugar and shortening until fluffy.
- Whisk eggs together in a bowl and add to mixture.
- In a separate bowl, sift flour, salt, and baking powder.
- Add flour mixture, alternately with milk, beginning and ending with flour mixture.
- Gently stir in blueberries.
- Pour into muffin tins filling ¾ way to the top.
- Bake for 15 minutes if using mini muffin pans, 35–40 if using regular size muffin pan.

Note: This batter will keep in the refrigerator for up to 1 week. Store in an airtight container and use as needed for fresh, hot muffins.

# "Fruitini"

*Juice of 2 lemons*
*Confectioners' sugar*
*Your favorite fresh fruit—*
   *cantaloupes*
   *kiwi*
   *strawberries*
   *bananas*
   *oranges*
   *grapes*
*Your favorite stemmed glass*

- Make balls out of melons. Slice kiwi, strawberries, bananas, and grapes. Section oranges. Mix together in a bowl.

- Dip rim of glasses into a shallow bowl of lemon juice.

- Put confectioners' sugar in bowl and dip rim of glass into confectioners' sugar.

- Fill the glasses with the fresh fruit.

- Top with a sprinkle of confectioners' sugar.

- Serve.

## Kid Notes

» Squeeze all of the juice out of the lemons—it's okay if some seeds are in the juice.

» Use a flick-of-the-wrist when using the melon baller.

» Use a plastic knife or a table knife to slice the fruit.

» Sprinkle the confectioners' sugar on top.

» Helpful hint: Here is how to get the most juice out of your lemon. Halve your lemon, place in microwave. Heat on high for 20 seconds.

# Kitchen Notes

# lazy morning brunch

Lazy mornings are a welcome and delicious reprieve from the hectic pace of our everyday lives. This breakfast or brunch menu is guaranteed to coax even the grumpiest "sleepyhead" out of bed. Our delicious Oven Baked French Toast is put together the night before so it can be popped in the oven the next morning. Grits are a traditional Southern favorite, but every transplanted Southerner who has served Cheddar Cheese Grits Casserole far away from home has won new converts. When Helen and her son Martin found themselves "grit-less" in Southern California, her family sent them by Federal Express. Absolutely Delicious Danish is a specialty of Leslie's sister Kim, who never goes to a family gathering without these, and Lazy Morning Muffins were a signature dish during Helen's years as a caterer in Dallas. The batter can be kept in the refrigerator and used as needed.

Overnight Oven Baked French Toast

Crispy Brown Sugar Bacon

Cheddar Cheese Grits Casserole

Absolutely Delicious Danish

Lazy Morning Muffins

# Overnight Oven Baked French Toast

*¼ cup butter*
*12 ¾-inch thick slices of French bread*
*6 eggs, beaten*
*1½ cups milk*
*¼ cup sugar*
*2 tablespoons maple syrup*
*1 teaspoon vanilla extract*
*½ teaspoon salt*
*Powdered sugar*

## Yield: 6 servings

- Lightly butter one side of the bread. Place the buttered bread in a 9- by 13-inch ovenproof glass pan, butter side up.

- Mix the eggs, milk, sugar, syrup, vanilla, and salt in a bowl and pour the mixture over the bread, turning the slices to coat. (Butter side will be down now.)

- Cover with foil and refrigerate overnight.

- Preheat oven to 400°.

- Bake until golden brown, about 40–45 minutes, turning the bread to bake evenly.

- Sprinkle with powdered sugar and serve.

## Kid Notes

» You put this delicious morning dish together the night before.

» Crack the eggs. (see Kid Notes on page 63)

» Use a whisk to blend the eggs, milk, sugar, syrup, and vanilla.

» Wake up and bake!

# Crispy Brown Sugar Bacon

*1 pound regular sliced bacon, room temperature*
*1 cup light brown sugar, firmly packed*
*1 tablespoon cracked black pepper (optional)*

## Yield: 6–8 servings

- Preheat oven to 425°.
- Line sheet pan with aluminum foil.
- Cut each slice of bacon in half.
- Mix brown sugar and pepper in a shallow bowl.
- Thoroughly coat each slice of the bacon with brown sugar mixture.
- Twist and place on sheet pan.
- Bake for 20–25 minutes until crisp.
- Cool on foil.
- Serve at room temperature.

## Kid Notes

» Ask an adult to turn the oven on for you.

» Wash your hands well after handling and twisting the bacon.

# Cheddar Cheese Grits Casserole

*1 quart milk*
*¼ cup butter*
*1 cup uncooked grits*
*1 teaspoon salt*
*½ teaspoon ground pepper*
*1 egg*
*8 ounces sharp cheddar cheese, grated*
*½ cup Parmesan cheese, grated*

## Yield: 6 servings

- Preheat oven to 350°.

- Grease a 2-quart casserole dish.

- Slowly bring milk to a boil over medium heat. Add butter and stir until melted.

- Add grits. Cook, stirring constantly, until mixture is the consistency of oatmeal (about 5–7 minutes).

- Remove from heat.

- Add salt, pepper, and egg. Whisk until well combined.

- Stir in cheddar cheese with a wooden spoon.

- Pour into a greased 2-quart casserole dish.

- Sprinkle with Parmesan cheese. Bake for 35–40 minutes.

## Kid Notes

» Crack the egg (see Kid Notes on page 63).

» Spy on the milk when it is heating on the stove— you don't want it to bubble over.

» The grits are hot! Be careful when stirring in the cheese.

# Absolutely Delicious Danish

*2 8-ounce cans crescent dinner rolls*
*16 ounces cream cheese, softened*
*1½ cups sugar, divided*
*1 egg*
*1 teaspoon vanilla extract*
*1 teaspoon almond extract*
*½ cup butter, melted*
*1 teaspoon ground cinnamon*
*1 cup almonds, chopped (optional)*

## Yield: 8–12 servings

- Preheat oven to 350°.

- Grease a 9- by 13-inch baking dish.

- Unroll one can crescent rolls and press into bottom of dish, pressing perforations together to form flat sheet of dough.

- Press edges of dough slightly up sides of dish.

- Put cream cheese, 1 cup of the sugar, egg, vanilla extract, and almond extract in a mixing bowl.

- Beat until smooth.

- Pour into pan and spread over crescent roll dough.

- Open remaining can of crescent rolls and place over cream cheese mixture, pinching perforations together. Press edges together to seal.

- Combine melted butter, remaining ½ cup sugar, cinnamon, and almonds.

- Spread evenly over top layer of crescent roll dough.

- Bake about 30 minutes or until golden.

- Cool for at least 20 minutes before cutting.

- To serve, cut into triangles or rectangles.

## Kid Notes

» Tear all of the paper off the cans of crescent rolls. Then bang on counter to open.

» Press the little "dots" together in the dough when it is in the pan.

» Crack the egg (see Kid Notes on page 63).

» Measure out 1 cup of sugar, then measure ½ cup sugar and put in a safe spot.

» To cut into triangles, first cut into squares, then cut the square on the diagonal.

# Lazy Morning Muffins

4 ½ cups flour
2 ½ cups sugar
2 tablespoons cinnamon
1 teaspoon salt
4 teaspoons baking soda
1 cup coconut
½ cup nuts (optional)
1 cup raisins
6 eggs
2 ¼ cups oil
2 tablespoons vanilla
2 cups mashed fruit (bananas, peaches, strawberries, apples)

## Yield: 3 dozen

- Preheat oven to 350°.
- Line muffin pan with muffin liners or grease muffin pan.
- Sift together flour, sugar, cinnamon, salt, and baking soda. Set aside.
- In a large bowl, mix eggs, oil, and vanilla.
- Add sifted ingredients. Mix well.
- Blend in coconut, nuts, and raisins.
- Fold in fruit.
- Fill muffin pans ¾ full.
- Bake for 15–18 minutes.

## Kid Notes

» Line or grease the muffin tins.

» Measure the dry ingredients and sift into a bowl.

» Crack the eggs (see Kid Notes on page 63).

» Mix the eggs, oil, and vanilla with a whisk.

» Remember how to fold ingredients (see Kid Notes on page 131).

# Kitchen Notes

# make and take picnic lunch!

Picnics celebrate good weather and good times and enhance our sense of fun and adventure. Packing a picnic lunch can be an adventure, too. We believe in "surprise sandwiches" (who said they had to be square?), and one of our favorites is the wrap. Wraps are versatile and can be easily loaded with any favorite filling. Cold soup is a great way to cool off a hot-weather picnic, and the kids love to help by pushing the "pulse" button on the blender. Watermelon cookies look just like the real thing, and of course, Mud 'N Worms are always a popular treat. These can be made by young cooks with very little supervision. They enjoy crushing the Oreos, stirring the filling, placing it in the cookie cups and of course—amid lots of squealing—sticking the worm in!

"Ice Chest" Strawberry Soup

Greek Wraps

Buffalo Chicken Wraps with Yummy Blue Cheese Dip

Chinese Chicken Wraps

Gouda Pimento Cheese Wraps

Of Course, Peanut Butter and Jelly Wraps

Veggie Fingers with Spicy Comeback Dip

Mud 'N Worms

Watermelon Cookies

# "Ice Chest" Strawberry Soup

*5 cups strawberries, washed, sliced, and hulled*
*½ cup sugar, or more to taste, depending on*
*    sweetness of strawberries*
*1 cup half and half*
*1 teaspoon almond extract*
*1 cup sour cream*

## Yield: 6–8 servings

- Put ingredients in blender. Puree until blended.

- Chill until ready to use.

- Put in thermos and take on picnic.

- Pour into small bowls and enjoy.

## Kid Notes

» Hulling strawberries means to take the stem out. Hold the pointed side with one hand and pinch across the top part.

» Measure the ingredients directly into the blender.

» Make sure the top is on tightly before you turn on the blender.

» You can "drink" your soup from a pretty glass or use a spoon.

# Greek Wraps

### Dressing:
½ cup plain yogurt
2 tablespoons lemon juice
1 tablespoon white wine vinegar
½ teaspoon dried oregano
½ teaspoon salt
½ garlic clove, chopped
½ teaspoon pepper
½ teaspoon Greek seasoning

### Filling:
6 chicken breasts, cooked
2 cups romaine lettuce, torn
1 cup tomatoes, diced
½ cup cucumber, diced
½ cup feta cheese, crumbled
¼ cup ripe olives, sliced
¼ cup purple onion, chopped
10–12 soft flour tortillas

Yield: 10–12 servings

- Put all dressing ingredients in a bowl and whisk. Set aside.

- Chop chicken breasts; put in bowl with other filling ingredients.

- Toss with dressing.

- Place one tortilla on a work surface and spread ½ cup of the mixture down the center.

- Roll up into a tight cylinder. Repeat with the remaining ingredients and serve.

# Buffalo Chicken Wraps with Yummy Blue Cheese Dressing

## Filling:
6 boneless, skinless chicken breasts
2 tablespoons butter, melted
6 tablespoons olive oil, divided
4 teaspoons Tabasco sauce
1 teaspoon Creole seasoning
1 teaspoon salt
1 teaspoon pepper
¼ teaspoon cayenne pepper
½ cup orange juice
1 tablespoon Dijon mustard
1 teaspoon sugar
1½ cups celery, shredded
1½ cups carrots, shredded
2 cups cucumber, diced and drained on
    paper towels

## Yummy Blue Cheese Dressing:
½ cup sour cream
¼ cup mayonnaise
½ cup blue cheese, crumbled
1 teaspoon cider vinegar
1 teaspoon fresh lemon juice
Dash Tabasco sauce
½ teaspoon onion, finely minced
Pinch garlic, finely chopped
Salt and pepper, to taste
12 soft flour tortillas

Yield: 12 servings

- Rinse chicken breast and pat dry. Place in a large bowl.

- In a small bowl, mix the melted butter, 2 tablespoons olive oil, Tabasco sauce, and Creole seasoning.

- Pour over chicken and coat evenly. Marinate, covered, at room temperature for 30 minutes.

- Heat grill to high.

- Combine salt, pepper, sugar, cayenne pepper, orange juice, Dijon mustard, and remaining 4 tablespoons olive oil.

- Place chicken on the grill and baste with the orange juice mixture. Cook turning once about 4–5 minutes per side until nicely charred on the outside and cooked through. (May take longer for larger breasts.)

- Remove chicken from the grill. Cool until able to touch, and slice into strips.

## Kid Notes

» Put each filling ingredient in a small bowl.

» Take a small Ziploc bag and put what you want in the bag.

» Add about 1 tablespoon dressing.

» Zip bag closed and shake.

» Open bag, put filling in tortilla, and roll up.

» Enjoy!

- Put chicken, celery, carrots, and cucumbers in a bowl and toss with Yummy Blue Cheese Dressing.
- Place one tortilla on a work surface and spread ½ cup mixture down the center.
- Roll into a tight cylinder. Repeat with remaining ingredients and serve.

### Yummy Blue Cheese Dressing:

- Combine sour cream and mayonnaise in a bowl.
- Fold in the blue cheese, then the remaining ingredients.
- This will keep 3 days in the refrigerator.

# Chinese Chicken Wraps

## Filling:

1 6-ounce package slivered almonds
¼ cup sesame seeds
1 package ramen noodles, crushed
2 tablespoons butter
6 cooked chicken breasts, shredded
½ head iceberg lettuce, shredded
4 green onions, chopped
¼ cup cilantro, chopped

## Dressing:

2 tablespoons sesame oil
¼ cup rice vinegar
¼ cup soy sauce
1 teaspoon salt
½ teaspoon pepper
1 teaspoon sugar
1 tablespoon garlic chili sauce
10–12 soft flour tortillas

Yield: 10–12 servings

- Sauté almonds, sesame seeds, and crushed ramen noodles in 2 tablespoons butter until brown, about 4–5 minutes.

- Place all filling ingredients into a large bowl.

- Place all dressing ingredients into another bowl and whisk.

- Pour dressing over filling ingredients and toss until thoroughly combined.

- Place one tortilla on a work surface and spread ½ cup filling down the center.

- Roll up into a tight cylinder. Repeat with remaining ingredients and serve.

## Kid Notes

» Wash the lettuce; lay on paper towels and pat dry.

» Ask for help when sautéing the almonds and sesame seeds.

» Squish the package of ramen noodles to break them up before sautéing them.

## Kid Notes

» Take a hunk of cheese and rub it downward on the grater, using the side with the larger holes. Be careful not to grate your fingers. You can also use a food processor to grate with adult supervision.

» Using the side of the grater with the smoother holes, grate the onion and save the juice that comes with it.

» If you love cheddar cheese more than anything in this world, it will work too!

» This spread is also great for sandwiches. You'll like them even better when you use your favorite cookie cutter to stamp out the sandwiches!

## Kid Notes

» You'll be surprised at how tasty the raisins or craisins make this, but you can leave them out if you want to.

» If you are allergic to peanut butter, you can use cream cheese.

# Gouda Pimento Cheese Wraps

2 pounds of Gouda (or smoked Gouda) cheese,
    coarsely grated
2 3-ounce jars of pimento, drained and diced
1¼ cups mayonnaise
1 small white onion, grated (save juice)
1 teaspoon black pepper
Pinch of salt
10-12 soft tortillas

## Yield: 10-12 wraps

▪ Put all ingredients, except tortillas, in a mixing bowl.

▪ Mix thoroughly by folding with a spatula.

▪ Spread the mixture on the tortilla and roll up.

▪ Left over Gouda Pimento Cheese may be stored in a covered container for up to one week.

# Of Course, Peanut Butter and Jelly Wraps

½ cup dried fruit bits (raisins or craisins)
½ cup peanut butter
⅛ teaspoon cinnamon
¼ cup your favorite jelly
6 soft flour tortillas

## Yield: 6 wraps

▪ In a small bowl, combine fruit bits, peanut butter, and cinnamon; mix well.

▪ Spread mixture evenly over tortillas. Dot with jelly. Roll up.

# Veggie Fingers with Spicy Comeback Sauce

*Carrots*
*Celery*
*English cucumbers*
*Black olives, whole*
*Cherry tomatoes, whole*

- Peel carrots.

- Wash celery.

- Peel cucumbers.

- Wash cherry tomatoes.

- Drain olives.

- Cut carrots, celery, and cucumbers into strips, about 3½ inches long and ¼ inch wide.

- Pack in separate containers for your picnic.

## To Assemble:

- Make a little hole on the end of the tomato with the tip of a sharp knife.

- Stick black olives or tomatoes on the tip of carrot, celery, or cucumber stick.

- Have fun making these "dippers" and dipping them in the Spicy Comeback Sauce.

## Kid Notes

» This is one recipe that you can do almost all by yourself—start to finish!

» Wash, peel, and cut the veggies. Then make them into funny fingers.

## Kid Notes

» Squeeze the lemons and make sure there are no seeds in the juice. (See Kid Notes Page 24.)

» Measure all of the ingredients directly into the blender.

» Pulsing means to quickly push the button on the blender and let go, then push again and let go, until it all looks blended.

# Spicy Comeback Sauce

3 cloves garlic, peeled
1 medium onion, chopped
½ cup ketchup
½ cup chili sauce
½ cup oil
1 tablespoon paprika
1 tablespoon Worcestershire sauce
2 tablespoons fresh lemon juice
1 teaspoon dry mustard
1½ teaspoons Creole seasoning
1 cup mayonnaise

### Yield: 3 cups

- Place ingredients in blender and pulse until blended.

- Store in the fridge for up to 2 weeks. It's great as a salad dressing too.

# Mud 'N Worms

### Mud Cups:
*¼ cup butter*
*½ cup sugar*
*¼ teaspoon vanilla*
*1 large egg*
*1 cup all-purpose flour*
*3 tablespoons cocoa*
*⅛ teaspoon salt*

### Filling:
*Instant chocolate pudding mix (4-serving size)*
*½ cup sour cream*
*1 cup cold milk*
*½ cup chocolate cookie crumbs*
*24 gummy worms*

Yield: 24 Mud 'n Worms

### Mud Cups:

- Cream butter and sugar until light and fluffy.

- Mix in vanilla and egg until well combined.

- Stir in flour, cocoa, and salt until dough forms a soft ball.

- Cover dough and refrigerate for 30 minutes.

- Divide into 24 portions. Roll into balls.

- Press individual balls into bottom and up sides of greased mini-muffin cups.

- Bake at 350° for 8–10 minutes until firm and set.

- Remove from the oven and lightly press the center down using a small spoon. Cool.

- Run point of sharp knife around top edge. Remove from pans.

## Kid Notes

» For cookie crumbs, you can put chocolate cookies in Ziploc bags and crush them with your fingers.

» If taking on a picnic, put pudding in a Ziploc and assemble when you are ready to serve. You can cut a small hole in bag and squeeze into cups.

» Creaming means to beat the butter and sugar together until it is fluffy. You can do this with a hand mixer or a standing mixer.

» Measure the sugar and the flour using a measuring cup for dry ingredients.

Continued —>

» Use a measuring spoon for the vanilla, cocoa, and salt.

» Crack the egg into a bowl (see Kid Notes on page 63).

» While the dough is refrigerating, grease 24 muffin cups.

» Have an adult assist when placing the muffin tins in the oven and taking out of the oven.

» For the filling, you will again use a mixer. Measure and add the sour cream and milk and beat for 1 minute on medium.

» A kitchen teaspoon works great for spooning in the filling.

## Filling:

- Beat pudding powder, sour cream, and cold milk together in medium bowl for about 1 minute until smooth.

- Spoon into mud cups.

- Sprinkle about 1 teaspoon cookie crumbs over each mud cup.

- Insert worm part way into filling.

# Watermelon Cookies

*3½ cups all-purpose flour, sifted*
*1½ teaspoons baking powder*
*1 teaspoon salt*
*1 cup butter*
*1½ cups sugar*
*1 tablespoon vanilla*
*2 eggs*
*red food coloring*
*1 package mini chocolate chips*
*2 cups powdered sugar*
*¼ cup water*
*green food coloring*

**Yield: 6–7 dozen cookies**

- Preheat the oven to 375°.

- Line baking sheet with parchment paper.

- Sift flour.

- Sift flour again with the baking powder and salt, and set aside.

- Cream butter, sugar, and vanilla.

- Add eggs and beat for 1 minute until fluffy. Slowly mix in the dry ingredients until blended.

- Add red food coloring to the dough. Add until the dough looks the color of watermelon.

- Cover with plastic wrap placed directly on the dough. Refrigerate for at least 30 minutes or overnight.

- Roll out cookie dough to ¼-inch thickness. Cut the cookies out with a round cookie cutter and then cut each one in half. (You may find it easier to cut in half on the baking sheet).

- Place on baking sheet.

- Place a few of the very small chocolate chips on each slice to make the "seeds."

- Bake about 8 minutes.

## Icing:

- Put powdered sugar and water in bowl and mix with green food coloring.

- You made need to add a little more powdered sugar or water to get preferred consistency.

- After the cookies have cooled roll the round edge in green icing. This makes each one look like a slice of watermelon.

## Kid Notes

» The recipe reads 3 ½ cups sifted flour—this means to sift the flour first and then measure. Sift again with the baking powder and salt.

» With a hand mixer or standing mixer, cream the butter, sugar, and vanilla until light and fluffy.

» When putting the food coloring in, add 1 drop at a time until it's your favorite watermelon color.

» Crack the eggs in a separate bowl (see Kid Notes on page 63).

» Roll cookie dough by placing a section of dough between 2 large sheets of wax or parchment paper. Use a rolling pin and roll over the top sheet, smoothing to about ¼-inch thickness. Peel away the top sheet and cut out the cookies with a cookie cutter. Use a spatula to transfer the cookies to a baking sheet.

» Scatter the mini chocolate chips on the cookie and gently press to look like watermelon seeds.

» Ask for help when placing the pan in and removing it from the oven.

# it's a school night supper!

The relentless dash from school to soccer practice to piano lessons is no excuse for fast-food school night suppers. This is a hearty meal that can be started ahead of time. The cheesy meatloaf can be mixed and assembled in the loaf pan, then covered and refrigerated for up to twenty-four hours until ready to bake. The carrots (once again, kids love to peel) can be cut into sticks and placed in a baggie in the fridge until ready to bake. The salad dressing and almonds for the salad will keep for up to two weeks. Hooray! for Hershey Bar Pie is a tasty incentive for finishing homework and can be made ahead of time and hidden away for the ultimate school night dessert. Any child that needs a study break can participate in the little preparation left for the night's meal. At the end of a full day of school and work, there is nothing better than a hot delicious supper for the family soul.

Cheesy Meatloaf

Carrot French Fries

Dynamite Orange Almond Salad

Creamed Corn

Parmesan Cheese Biscuits

Hooray! for Hershey Bar Pie

# Cheesy Meatloaf

¼ cup onion, finely chopped
½ cup celery, finely chopped
2 teaspoons garlic, minced
1 teaspoon dried parsley
2 teaspoons Creole seasoning
¼ teaspoon pepper
1 teaspoon chili powder
1 teaspoon cumin
¾ cup salsa
3 eggs
1½ pounds lean ground beef or a mix
   of lean ground beef and ground
   turkey
¾ cup bread crumbs
½ pound mozzarella cheese, sliced

### Yield: 8 servings

- Heat the oven to 350°.

- Place all ingredients, except cheese, in a large mixing bowl. Mix well with your hands.

- Transfer half the mixture to a 9- by 5-inch loaf pan. Place mozzarella slices on top, then cover with the rest of the meat mixture.

- Bake for 60–70 minutes, or until a meat thermometer reads 170°.

- Let meatloaf rest in pan for 20 minutes.

- Serve.

## Kid Notes

» Our kids put the vegetables in a mini-chopper for instant gratification/results.

» Be sure to wash your hands after mixing the meatloaf.

» If you don't have bread crumbs, put dry, stale bread in the mini-chopper and pulse until fine.

» Leftover meatloaf makes a great sandwich.

# Carrot French Fries

2 pounds carrots
3 tablespoons butter, melted
2 teaspoons fresh rosemary, finely
    chopped (optional)

½ teaspoon sugar
½ teaspoon salt
¼ teaspoon pepper

**Yield: 8 servings**

- Preheat oven to 425°. Line a jellyroll pan with parchment paper.

- Using a sharp knife and cutting board, cut away the tip and end of each carrot. Place 1 carrot on the board and hold with one hand. Holding the peeler in the other hand, run it over the carrot, always peeling away from you. Turn the carrot as needed to peel completely. Repeat with the other carrots.

- Using a sharp knife, cut 1 carrot in half crosswise. Next, cut each half in half lengthwise. Finally, cut each half in half lengthwise again. You will end up with 8 sticks from the carrot. Repeat with the other carrots.

- In the mixing bowl, combine the carrot sticks, butter, rosemary (if using), sugar, salt, and pepper. Stir with a rubber spatula until the carrot sticks are evenly coated with all the other ingredients.

- Dump the carrots onto the parchment-lined jellyroll pan. Spread the sticks out as much as possible. Bake until the carrots are tender and well browned, about 20 minutes. Using oven mitts, remove the pan from the oven. Serve the carrot fries hot or at room temperature.

## Kid Notes

» These are so good, you may want to "biggie-size!"

» Carrots are hard to cut. You do the peeling, and let an adult do the cutting. Remember to always scrape the peeler down the carrot.

» This is an easy recipe. You cannot mess up.

# Dynamite Orange Almond Salad

*½ teaspoon salt*
*Pepper, to taste*
*2 tablespoons sugar*
*4 tablespoons vinegar*
*¼ cup oil*
*6 drops Tabasco sauce*
*2 tablespoons fresh parsley, chopped*
*1 15-ounce can mandarin oranges, drained*
*½ cup almonds, sliced*
*3 tablespoons sugar*
*1 bag mixed greens*
*2 green onions, chopped*

### Yield: 6–8 servings

- For dynamite orange almond salad dressing, combine first seven ingredients (from salt to parsley). Whisk ingredients until well blended.

- For glazed almonds, combine almonds and sugar in a small skillet. Heat on low and stir constantly until sugar is dissolved and the almonds are well coated. Sugar can caramelize quickly and burn—watch carefully!

- Pour onto wax paper to cool.

- Once cooled, break into small pieces.

- To serve the salad, combine salad greens, chopped green onions, and mandarin orange slices in a large salad bowl.

- Pour dressing over salad and toss to combine.

- Sprinkle almonds on top and serve.

## Kid Notes

» You are going to love this salad. It's really dynamite to eat!

» Wash the lettuce and pat dry on paper towels.

» Use a whisk to mix the dressing ingredients. Be sure to add the ingredients in order.

» Wait until ready to serve to pour dressing on the salad. Then toss all together.

» Ask for help with glazing the almonds.

## Kid Notes

» If using fresh corn, show your parents how to shuck it!

» Place the corn on a cutting board and using a table knife cut downwards to scrape the kernels off of the cob.

» Ask for assistance when making the white sauce on the stove. Just stir with a whisk until creamy and thick.

# Creamed Corn

*2 tablespoons butter*
*½ onion, finely chopped*
*3 tablespoons flour*
*1¾ cups milk*
*2½ cups corn, fresh (4 or 5 ears, cut off the cob)*
*1 teaspoon sugar*
*Salt and pepper, to taste*

## Yield: 6–8 servings

- Melt the butter in a skillet and sauté the onion until translucent, about 5 minutes.

- Add flour and stir.

- With a wire whisk, gradually add the milk and cook over medium heat until thickened.

- Stir in corn, salt, pepper, and sugar.

- Serve warm.

# Parmesan Cheese Biscuits

*2 cups all-purpose flour, plus more as needed*
*¼ teaspoon baking soda*
*1 tablespoon baking powder*
*1 teaspoon salt*
*6 tablespoons shortening*
*¾ cup buttermilk*
*1 cup Parmesan cheese, shredded*

## Yield: 12 biscuits

- Preheat the oven to 400°.

- Sift the dry ingredients into a roomy bowl.

- Cut in the shortening with a pastry blender or fork until the mixture has the texture of coarse meal.

- Add the buttermilk and mix with a wooden spoon, lightly but thoroughly.

- Add a little more flour if the dough is too sticky.

- Add Parmesan cheese and knead dough gently.

- Roll the dough out ½ inch thick on a lightly floured surface or pastry cloth.

- Cut the dough using a 2-inch biscuit cutter.

- Place the biscuits on a baking sheet and bake until golden brown, 10–12 minutes.

## Kid Notes

» You can even use your fingers to "cut" the butter into the flour. The object is to rub the butter into the flour so that only little crumbs show through.

» Once rolled out, you can measure the dough with a ruler to make sure that it is close enough to the desired thickness.

» You can buy already shredded Parmesan or use a microplane to grate the cheese.

# Hooray! for Hershey Bar Pie

*6 Hershey bars with almonds*
*½ cup milk*
*20 large marshmallows*
*1 8-ounce carton Cool Whip*
*1 Chocolate Wafer Pie Crust (see page 180)*

## Yield: 6–9 servings

- Prepare Chocolate Wafer Pie Crust and set aside 2 tablespoons of the crushed Oreos or chocolate wafers to sprinkle over the top of the pie.

- Put milk and marshmallows in a saucepan on low heat, stirring constantly. When marshmallows are melted, add Hershey bars.

- Stir until melted and blended.

- Pour mixture into cooled pie crust.

- Refrigerate for at least 30 minutes.

- When pie is set, spread Cool Whip over the top.

- Sprinkle the Oreos that were set aside over the top.

## Kid Notes

» Plain Hershey bars work just as well.

» Use a wooden spoon to stir in the marshmallows.

» Use a spatula to smooth the Cool Whip all over the top.

# not so mundane
# monday night

We don't believe in "Mundane Mondays," so we get a jump on Monday night supper by planning ahead on Sunday. We collectively ease out of our weekend frame of mind by gently turning our attention toward the new week. During the school year, this means washing off the weekend with a good hot bath, collecting books, thinking about homework, and planning meals. For Monday's dinner, we start the night before by marinating the beef, trimming the Broccoli Trees, boiling the potatoes, and making the brownies. (We never mind if a brownie or two disappears or finds its way into a Monday lunch box.) We wait until just before supper to make the Golden Cheese Wedge biscuits. They're simple and fun to make—a tasty treat and reward for preparing a "not so mundane" Monday night dinner.

"Here's the Beef" Kebabs

Broccoli Trees

Volcano Potatoes

Golden Cheese Wedges

A+ Brownies

# "Here's the Beef" Kebabs

## Marinade:
2 cloves garlic, crushed
1 tablespoon sesame oil
1 teaspoon honey
1 tbsp. lemon juice
½ cup soy sauce

## Kebabs:
1½ pounds London broil or round cut,
    cut into 1-inch cubes
1 large green pepper, cored and cut
    into 1-inch pieces
1 large red pepper, cored and cut into
    1-inch pieces
5 small onions, sliced in half
10 fresh mushrooms
10 skewers
10 fresh rosemary sprigs or 2
    tablespoons dried rosemary leaves

Yield: 8–10 servings

### Kid Notes

» Use a garlic press to crush the garlic cloves.

» Ask an adult to cut the beef and onions—they require a sharp knife.

» You can cut the peppers using a plastic or table knife.

» Be careful when pushing the meat and vegetables on the skewer—there is a sharp point on the end.

» Ask an adult to help prepare the barbecue or a stove top grill.

- Place the meat in the marinade, cover, and refrigerate for at least 2 hours or overnight, turning the meat occasionally for an even coating. This may be done in a Ziploc bag.

- If using bamboo skewers, make sure to soak them in warm water for at least 30 minutes before using.

- Assemble the kebabs by alternately spearing the beef, peppers, onions, and mushrooms on skewers.

- Twist one rosemary sprig around each skewer, or sprinkle rosemary leaves all over in the marinade.

- Grill the kebabs, turning occasionally, until cooked to desired doneness.

## Kid Notes

» Be careful and use your good knife skills when cutting the broccoli into "trees."

» Get assistance when steaming and draining the hot broccoli.

# Broccoli Trees

*1 pound broccoli florets with 2-inch stems*
*Water*
*4 teaspoons Parmesan cheese, grated*
*2 teaspoons lemon pepper*

### Yield: 6 servings

- Peel any thick fibrous skin from broccoli stem. Cut "trees" by separating florets with knife and slicing down through stem.

- Place in steamer over simmering water. Cover. Steam for 8–10 minutes, until stems are tender and broccoli is bright green. Drain.

- Combine Parmesan cheese and seasoning in small dish. Sprinkle over broccoli.

# Volcano Potatoes

*6 large potatoes*
*4 tablespoons butter*
*1 teaspoon salt, more or less to desired taste*
*¼ teaspoon black pepper, more or less to desired taste*
*⅓ cup milk*
*2 egg yolks*
*Butter to grease baking dish*
*6 tablespoons cheddar cheese, grated*

## Yield: 6–8 servings

- Peel the potatoes, and then cut each potato into 4 pieces.

- Put the potatoes into a large saucepan and add enough cold water to cover them by 1 inch.

- Bring to a boil over high heat. Reduce the heat until the water simmers or bubbles slightly. Cover the saucepan and cook the potatoes for 20 minutes.

- After 20 minutes, insert the fork into a potato piece. If it goes in easily, the potatoes are done.

- Place the colander in the sink and drain the potatoes.

- Put the potatoes back into the saucepan. Add egg yolks to the potatoes while they are hot. Use a hand mixer or standing mixer to beat the potatoes and egg yolks until they are smooth.

- Add the butter, salt, pepper, and milk. Beat the potatoes with mixer until they are light and fluffy.

- Preheat oven to 350°. Lightly grease a medium baking dish with butter. Spoon 6–8 mounds of mashed potatoes, each about 3 inches high, into the baking dish.

- Use a rubber spatula to shape the potatoes into volcano shapes. Use a spoon to make a crater in the top of each volcano.

- Fill each volcano with a tablespoon of the grated cheese. Bake the volcano potatoes until the cheese melts and the potatoes are lightly browned.
- Remove potatoes from oven. Use a metal spatula to loosen the potatoes carefully from the bottom of the baking dish. Lift them directly onto each dinner plate and serve.

## Kid Notes

» Remember when peeling the potatoes to scrape the peeler down the potato toward the cutting board. Turn the potato as you need to in order to peel it all around.

» Have an adult take the hot pan of potatoes to the sink to pour the water through the colander.

» When using the electric hand mixer to blend the potatoes be sure to keep the beaters in the mixture until you turn the mixer off. Otherwise you will be wiping mashed potatoes off the kitchen cabinets and walls!

» Separating eggs is not a hard thing to do. Have two bowls ready. With one hand, tap the egg on the edge of the bowl to make an even crack. Then using both hands pull the edges apart until the whole egg is now in two parts. Some of the white will instantly fall into the bowl underneath you. That bowl is for egg whites only. Pour the rest of the egg back and forth from one half shell to the other, allowing egg white to fall into the egg-white-only bowl. When only yolk remains in the shell, pour it into the other bowl—the yolk-only bowl. Should you get yolk into the white, try to remove it with the corner of a paper towel.

» Ask an adult to assist you when placing Volcano Potatoes in the oven and taking them out.

» Use extra cheese on top if you'd like. Yum!

# Golden Cheese Wedges

*2 cups flour*
*1 tablespoon baking powder*
*¼ teaspoon salt*
*5 tablespoons cold butter*
*⅔ cup milk*
*½ cup cheddar cheese, shredded*

## Yield: 8 servings

- Preheat oven to 400°.

- Lightly grease a 9-inch pie plate.

- Combine the flour, baking powder, and salt in the bowl of a food processor or electric mixer. Add the butter in chunks, and pulse until the mixture resembles coarse meal.

- Add the milk and pulse until just combined.

- Turn the dough out onto a lightly floured surface, and pat into a round shape, about ⅓-inch thick. Place the round in the pie plate and cut into wedges, not cutting all the way through.

- Cover with the shredded cheese and bake for 15 minutes, or until lightly brown on the top and cooked through. If the cheese hasn't browned, broil for one minute.

## Kid Notes

» Pulse the ingredients in the food processor by making short, snappy pushes on the turn-on switch. Pulse only until the ingredients are combined.

» Use extra flour on your hands and the surface that you are patting the dough out on if it feels too sticky.

» Ask for help placing the wedges in and removing them from the oven.

» Enjoy while hot with extra butter (and jelly too)!

# A+ Brownies

1 cup butter
4 1-ounce squares unsweetened chocolate
4 eggs
2 teaspoons vanilla extract
2 cups sugar
½ teaspoon salt
½ teaspoon baking powder
1 cup flour
1 12-ounce package miniature chocolate chips

**Yield: 10–12 servings**

- Preheat oven to 325°. Grease a 9- by 11-inch pan and set aside.

- Slowly melt the butter and unsweetened chocolate over low heat in a double boiler, stirring occasionally. This can also be done in a microwave. Place butter and chocolate in a microwave-safe dish. Microwave for 1 minute. Check and stir. If not melted, continue to microwave in 30-second intervals until smooth.

- Put the eggs and vanilla extract in a mixing bowl and whisk.

- Add the sugar, salt, baking powder, and flour and blend with a hand mixer or standing mixer until combined.

- Carefully add the melted chocolate mixture. Mix until thoroughly blended.

- Fold in chocolate chips.

- Pour mixture into the prepared baking pan and bake for 25–30 minutes, or until a toothpick inserted in the center of brownies comes out clean.

- Let cool and cut into squares.

## Kid Notes

» Ask an adult to help you melt the chocolate and butter. Remind your helper to do so over low heat so as not to scorch the chocolate.

» When cracking the eggs, use a separate bowl. With one hand tap the egg on the side of the bowl.

» Using both hands, pull the edges apart and let the egg fall into the bowl. If any shell falls in, remove by pushing it to the side of the bowl with a paper towel.

» Ask for help when placing the brownies in and removing them from the oven.

» Make an A+ and you can have two brownies!

# ring the dinner bell

You won't have to ring the dinner bell for this fabulous family meal; the whole family will already be in the kitchen. Colorful, tasty, and nutritious, this menu is perfect for Sunday lunch or those special "company's coming" occasions. We have discovered time and time again in our cooking classes that children enjoy simple tasks like peeling carrots and stirring that adults find monotonous. In the never-ending search for "something new," Leslie tried Parmesan Risotto for her family and they loved it. They loved helping, too. Risotto requires lots of stirring. And it's not only an important job; kids feel important doing it. The Buttermilk Pie is a particular favorite of Leslie's son, Myers, and the wonderful aroma of Grandmother's Rolls evokes fond memories for Helen. The rolls are easy to make with the dough prepared the night before. Unlike grownups, children are not the least bit intimidated by working with dough. They especially love to watch it rise.

Tasty, Tender Pork Tenderloin

Carrot Coins

Creamy Dreamy Broccoli Parmesan Risotto

Grandmother's Dinner Rolls

Myer's Favorite Buttermilk Pie

# Tasty, Tender Pork Tenderloin

3 tablespoons soy sauce
3 tablespoons hoisin sauce
2 tablespoons oil
1½ teaspoons sugar
1½ pounds pork tenderloin
2 tablespoons butter
1 quart Ziploc bag

## Yield: 6 servings

- Put tenderloin in Ziploc bag. Add soy sauce, hoisin sauce, oil, salt, and sugar. Marinate tenderloin in the refrigerator for at least 2 hours.

- Preheat oven to 500°.

- Put tenderloin in roasting pan.

- Place in very hot (500°) oven for 9 minutes.

- Turn meat, roast 9 minutes more.

- Slice meat across the grain into thin slices.

- Add butter to pan drippings and stir well.

- Drizzle over meat.

## Kid Notes

» Measure the marinade ingredients.

» Wash your hands thoroughly after marinating the pork.

» Pork can even marinate overnight.

» Ask for assistance when placing the pork in and taking out of the oven and turning it.

» This cut of pork has very little fat and is very tender, so it cooks well at this high temperature.

# Carrot Coins

*10–12 medium-long, thin carrots, peeled and sliced into thin rounds*
*2 tablespoons butter*
*½ teaspoon salt*
*¼ teaspoon pepper*
*2 teaspoons orange juice*
*2 tablespoons light brown sugar*
*½ cup water*
*2 teaspoons sesame seeds, toasted*

## Yield: 6–8 portions

- Preheat oven to 375°.

- Boil or steam carrots in water until tender but not mushy, about 10 minutes.

- Drain carrots in a colander.

- While the carrots are cooking, you can toast the sesame seeds. Spread the sesame seeds on a sheet pan and toast for 5 minutes.

- After carrots are cooked, sprinkle sesame seeds on top.

- Add all ingredients to the pan.

- Cook and stir over medium heat until the carrots are nicely coated with syrup.

- Add more sugar and/or water, depending on how syrupy you like it.

## Kid Notes

» When peeling the carrots always scrape in a downward motion and turn the carrot as needed.

» You will need assistance in using a sharp knife to cut the carrots into coins.

» Ask for help when draining the carrot coins and putting them back on the stove.

» Measure ingredients, pour into saucepan, and stir until syrupy and thickened.

# Creamy Dreamy Broccoli Parmesan Risotto

*6 cups chicken broth, heated*
*1 onion, finely chopped*
*3 tablespoons olive oil*
*1½ cups rice, uncooked, short-grained (Arborio) or*
*medium-grained regular rice*
*2 cups broccoli, cut into florets*
*1½ cups Parmesan cheese, grated*
*½ teaspoon salt*

## Yield: 6–8 servings

- In a heavy saucepan, sauté finely chopped onion in olive oil until transparent in color. Add the rice and cook over medium-high heat, stirring constantly for about 2 minutes.

- Reduce heat to medium-low and add 1 cup of the warm broth. Stir until completely absorbed by rice. Continue to add the warm broth, 1 cup at a time, constantly stirring, saving 1 cup for the end.

- Once the 5 cups of broth have been thoroughly absorbed, stir in the broccoli and the final cup of broth. Stir, stir, and stir for 5 minutes.

- Add 1½ cups Parmesan cheese and salt. The risotto should be creamy in consistency. Allow to stand for a minute or two, then, enjoy.

Time saver: Buy pre-grated Parmesan cheese.

## Kid Notes

» Ask for help when using a sharp knife to chop the onions and cut the broccoli.

» This recipe requires a lot of stirring—almost constantly for about 20–25 minutes. But when it is ready, prepare your taste buds for a treat!

» You can grate the Parmesan, or buy it already shredded.

# Grandmother's Dinner Rolls

2 cups milk
½ cup sugar
½ cup vegetable shortening
¼ cup water (105°–115°)
1 package active dry yeast
4 cups all-purpose flour
1 teaspoon baking soda
1 teaspoon salt
1 teaspoon baking powder

**Yield: About 5 dozen rolls**

## Kid Notes

» Just heat the milk and shortening until the shortening melts—no boiling here. The milk and shortening should feel like a baby's bath.

» Measure the dry ingredients and sift together.

» The secret to these rolls is in refrigerating the covered dough overnight.

» These rolls always turn out good and are the hit of the meal!

- In a small pan on top of stove, melt sugar and shortening in milk. Cool.

- Dissolve yeast in water.

- When milk mixture cools, transfer it to a bowl. Add yeast and 2 cups flour.

- Beat with hand mixer or wooden spoon to get out the lumps.

- Cover with a clean dish towel and let rise 45 minutes in a warm place.

- Sift 1½ cups flour, baking soda, salt, and baking powder. Add to the risen yeast and flour mixture.

- Place dough in refrigerator, covered, overnight until ready to use.

- Place dough on floured board or counter top.

- Work additional flour into the sticky dough until it is the right consistency for rolling out.

- With a floured rolling pin, roll out dough to a ½-inch thickness. Cut rounds with a biscuit cutter, fold over and place in a greased pan or cookie sheet. Let rise covered for 20 minutes before baking.

- Bake at 400° until done, about 10–12 minutes.

- Serve warm with honey or butter.

# Myer's Favorite Buttermilk Pie

*1 9-inch pie crust (see page 181)*
*1¼ cups sugar*
*½ cup butter, room temperature*
*1 tablespoon flour*
*3 eggs, well beaten*
*¾ cup buttermilk*
*1 tablespoon vanilla extract*

## Yield: 8 servings

- Preheat oven to 500°.

- Prepare pie crust according to directions, or use a ready-made pie crust.

- Blend sugar, butter, and flour using a mixer on low speed.

- Add eggs, vanilla extract, and buttermilk. Mix until combined.

- Pour into pie crust. Turn oven to 400°.

- Place pie in oven and bake at 400° for 10 minutes.

- Without opening the oven door, reduce temperature to 325° and bake for an additional 40–45 minutes.

- Allow to cool before serving.

## Kid Notes

» You can use a hand mixer or standing mixer for blending.

» Crack the eggs (see Kid Notes on page 63). Whisk until foamy.

» Measure the ingredients.

» Remember to use liquid measuring cup for measuring the buttermilk.

» Pour pie mixture into pie crust.

» Use a timer to help you remember when to change the degree of the oven temperature. (It changes three times for this pie!)

# Kitchen Notes

# everyone, sit down for dinner

One of our most enthusiastic students in "Kids in the Kitchen" classes is a blue-eyed five-year-old named Sterling who claims that her father makes the best roasted chicken in the whole wide world. Helen happily accepted an invitation to watch this father-daughter duo make the ultimate comfort food. Sterling reached in a low kitchen drawer and found aprons for each of them. She then pulled up a stool and helped her father, Clark, find the seasonings. He held the chicken over the sink and she seasoned it, layering the seasonings evenly before helping put the bird in the roasting pan. It was unmistakably apparent (and not only to her proud cooking teacher) that both Sterling and her father were "at home" in the family kitchen and had prepared this dish many times before. And we agree with Sterling, the best roasted chicken in the whole wide world is made when families cook together.

Wholesome Roasted Chicken

Sensational Succotash

Martin's Baked Sweet Potatoes

Cornbread Gems

Heavenly Butterfinger Dessert

# Wholesome Roasted Chicken

*1 whole chicken (4–7 pounds)*

| | |
|---|---|
| *Olive oil* | *Red pepper* |
| *Tabasco* | *Paprika* |
| *Salt* | *Garlic powder* |
| *Black pepper* | *Season-all or any season salt* |
| *Lemon pepper* | *Rosemary* |

### Yield: 4–6 servings

- Preheat oven to 325°. Position a rack in the center of the oven.

- Cover bottom of ovenproof glass baking dish with olive oil. Put 8–10 drops of Tabasco in olive oil. Stir mixture. (This zips up the olive oil.)

- Remove the giblets and the neck from inside of the chicken and discard. Rinse and lightly pat dry the chicken. You want chicken damp so that the seasonings stick to the chicken.

- Hold chicken over the sink, breast down and begin seasoning the back first.

- The order of the seasonings is very important.

- Dust the chicken evenly and lightly with each seasoning beginning with the salt and continuing in this order: black pepper, red pepper, paprika, garlic powder, lemon pepper, Season-all.

- When you finish covering with the Season-all, all the skin color of this chicken should have disappeared. Shake a little lemon pepper and rosemary in the olive oil mixture. Lay the seasoned side down (which is the back) in the pan with the olive oil mixture.

- Repeat layering with the seasonings on the front side. Make sure you pull and get around the legs. Top off with rosemary. Cover with aluminum foil.

- Put in the oven for 1 hour and 45 minutes, or until the juices run clear. After 1 hour, baste the chicken. (You can never over baste.) Remove foil for the last 15 minutes of cooking to produce a crispy glazed skin.

## Kid Notes

» Line your seasonings in order before you begin dusting the chicken with them.

» Enjoy the smell of your kitchen while this chicken is roasting! Delicious!

» You will have time to make the rest of your dinner while it cooks.

# Sensational Succotash

*1½ cups fresh or frozen corn kernels*
*1½ cups fresh or frozen lima beans*
*1 tablespoon butter*
*½ teaspoon salt*
*¼ teaspoon pepper*
*⅓ cup half and half*

## Yield: 6–8 servings

- Put the lima beans in a medium saucepan with 3 cups of water. Bring to a boil, reduce the heat, cover, and simmer for about 10 minutes.

- Turn heat back on high and add the corn. When beans and corn have come to a boil, reduce heat to low and simmer, covered, for 5 more minutes. Remove from heat and drain in a colander.

- Melt 1 tablespoon butter in a heavy skillet. Add the beans, corn, salt, and pepper. Stir to combine. Pour in half and half and simmer slowly for about 15 more minutes.

## Kid Notes

» Ask for assistance when using the stove top to cook the lima beans and the corn.

» If using fresh corn, you'll need a sharp knife to cut the kernels off of the cob—have an adult help.

# Martin's Baked Sweet Potatoes

*6 large sweet potatoes*
*4 tablespoons unsalted butter*
*2 teaspoons kosher salt*

## Yield: 6 servings

- Preheat the oven to 400°.

- Wash sweet potatoes.

- Pierce them with a fork and wrap in aluminum foil. (For faster cooking, cut potatoes in large cubes and wrap in aluminum foil.)

- Place sweet potatoes on a baking sheet and bake until easily pierced with a fork, about 1 hour.

- Peel the sweet potatoes while still hot.

- Combine the sweet potatoes, butter, and salt in a large bowl. Mash with a potato masher until the potatoes are smooth. Serve immediately. (This can be prepared a day ahead and reheated).

## Kid Notes

» You can do this almost all by yourself!

» Ask for help when placing in and removing from the oven.

» Be careful when peeling the hot potatoes.

## Kid Notes

» Sift all of the dry ingredients together after measuring with a dry measuring cup.

» Pour the milk into a liquid measuring cup and add.

» Crack egg (see Kids Notes on page 63).

» The butter can be melted in the microwave. Place in a glass dish and heat for about 20 seconds.

# Cornbread Gems

½ cup yellow cornmeal
1 cup all-purpose flour
3 teaspoons baking powder
2 tablespoons sugar
1 teaspoon salt
¾ cup milk
1 egg, beaten
2 tablespoons butter, melted

## Yield: 1 dozen

- Preheat oven to 425°.

- Grease muffin tins.

- Sift together all of the dry ingredients.

- Gradually add milk, stirring well.

- Add beaten egg. Then, blend in melted butter.

- Pour into muffin tins and bake for 15 minutes.

# Heavenly Butterfinger Dessert

*16 ounces angel food cake*
*6 Butterfinger candy bars*
*1 pint whipping cream*
*¼ cup butter, melted*
*2 eggs*
*2 teaspoons vanilla extract*
*2 cups powdered sugar*

### Yield: 10–12 servings

- In a medium mixing bowl beat the eggs with a whisk until blended.

- Pour melted butter over the eggs and whisk again until blended. (The hot butter will cook the eggs.)

- Add the sugar and blend until smooth. Whisk in the vanilla extract.

- Using a hand mixer, whip the whipping cream until stiff.

- Fold the whipped cream into the egg and butter mixture.

- Break the angel food cake into small pieces.

- Crush the Butterfingers by pulsing in a food processor or by placing in a Ziploc bag and rolling with a rolling pin.

- In a 9- by 13-inch pan, layer half of the angel food cake pieces, half of the creamed mixture, and half of the Butterfingers. Repeat. Cover and refrigerate overnight.

Note: You may also use a trifle bowl.

## Kid Notes

» Crack the eggs into a bowl (see Kid Notes on page 63).

» For best results: make sure that the whipping cream is cold and that the mixing bowl and beaters are chilled (by placing in the freezer for 10 minutes) for the best results. Beat continuously with a standing mixer or a hand mixer at medium speed until the cream begins to stiffen. Be careful not to overbeat the cream because it will fall and become soupy.

» You can tear the angel food cake into small pieces with your fingers.

» Crush the butterfingers.

# Kitchen Notes

# it's italian!

Why not make your next special family night an Italian extravaganza? Everyone gets a job, and in a little over an hour, each dish comes together and is ready to serve. Making pasta is family fun at its finest—even for the most reluctant teenager. With an inexpensive hand-crank pasta machine, easy, made-from-scratch pasta dough goes from a ball to long, thin strands in a matter of minutes. While your dough is resting, make the rest of the menu. Choose from two delicious sauces, whip up a classic Caesar Salad with Homemade Croutons, bake a loaf of Crusty Italian Bread, and top it all off with a super-delicious and super-easy Totally Terrific Tiramisu.

Homemade Pasta Dough
Unrivaled Red Sauce with Mighty Meatballs
Favorite Fettuccine Alfredo
Caesar Salad with Homemade Croutons
Crusty Italian Bread
Totally Terrific Tiramisu

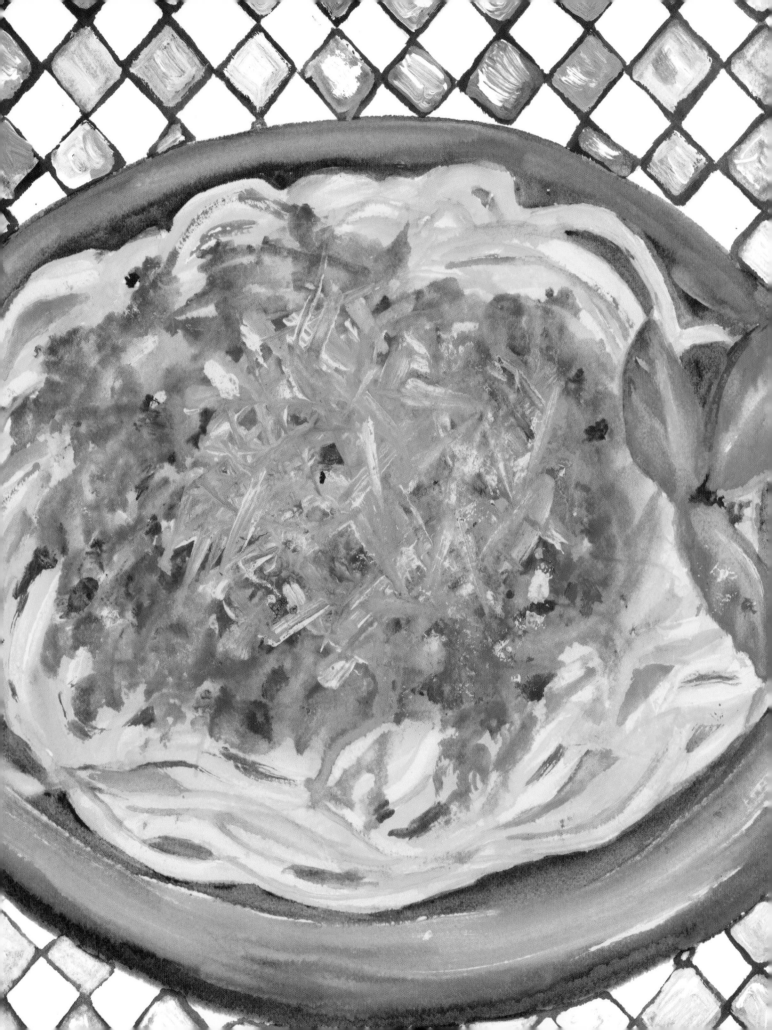

# Homemade Pasta Dough

*3 cups white bread flour*
*4 large eggs, room temperature*
*1 teaspoon salt*
*1 tablespoon olive oil*
*Pasta machine*

**Yield: Enough pasta for 6–8 servings (double amounts for lasagna)**

- Place the flour and salt in a bowl, and make a well in the center.

- Beat the eggs. Pour into the well in the center of the flour.

- Mix with a fork at first, then flour one of your hands, and knead the dough until it is uniform and smooth, about 5 minutes. Add a little more flour if the dough seems unreasonably sticky.

- Cover the dough with a clean dishtowel, and let it rest at room temperature for 1 hour.

- After the pasta dough has rested, turn it out onto a lightly floured surface, and knead it for about 1 minute.

- Divide the dough into balls the size of a tight fist.

- Begin feeding through the pasta machine following the steps to make a long sheet.

- Run the dough through the cutting mode and cut into long thin strands for spaghetti or slightly thicker strands for fettuccine. (Alternately, you may cut the dough into any shape you like. For lasagna you can either leave the sheets whole or cut into long, wide noodles—you name it!)

- Cook pasta in a large saucepan with lightly salted boiling water until just done, about 5 minutes. Be careful not to overcook! Homemade pasta cooks much more quickly than the dried kind! Pour pasta into a collander and drain.

Note: The pasta can be frozen after cutting into strands.

## Kid Notes

» See page 63 for egg-cracking instructions.

» Kneading converts the dough from being slightly sticky to more elastic. When you knead with your hands, rub them in a little flour first, then press the dough with the heel of your hand and fold it over and over itself. Start again forming it into a loose ball, then press and fold again. It takes about 5–10 minutes of this continuous motion to make the dough smooth and elastic.

» It is important that you allow the dough to rest after playing with it so hard. That way it will have energy to turn itself into food on your plate.

## Kid Notes

» You may chop the garlic or press the garlic through a garlic press. One clove of garlic equals ½ teaspoon of pressed garlic. For this recipe you will need 4 cloves. We love the garlic press!

» You can take charge of measuring the ingredients for this sauce, while an adult handles the actual cooking over the stove.

» Have fun dumping into the pot! Stir with a long-handled wooden spoon.

# Unrivaled Red Sauce

2 tablespoons olive oil
1½ cups yellow onion, finely chopped
2 teaspoons garlic, minced (4 cloves)
½ teaspoon salt
2 teaspoons Italian seasoning
¼ teaspoon ground black pepper
1 28-ounce can tomato puree
2 15-ounce cans tomato sauce
1 6-ounce can tomato paste
1½ cups water
1 teaspoon sugar

## Yield: 8 cups

- Heat the olive oil in a large, stock pot over medium heat.

- Add the onions, garlic, salt, Italian seasoning, and pepper and cook until onions are soft and clear, about 4 minutes.

- Place the tomato puree in stock pot. Stir with a wooden spoon.

- Add the tomato sauce, tomato paste, water, and sugar to the pot with the onion and stir well.

- Bring to a simmer over medium-high heat.

- Lower the heat to medium-low and simmer, uncovered, for 45 minutes, stirring occasionally with a long-handled wooden spoon.

- Using potholders, remove the pot from the heat and use the sauce as needed. Once it has cooled, you can store this sauce in an airtight container in the refrigerator for up to 4 days or freeze it up to 3 months.

# Mighty Meatballs

8 cups Unrivaled Red Sauce (see page 83)
2 large eggs
1½ pounds lean ground turkey or lean ground beef
½ cup yellow onion, finely chopped
1 teaspoon garlic, minced
2 teaspoons Italian seasoning
½ teaspoon ground black pepper
2 teaspoons yellow mustard
2 teaspoons ketchup
½ teaspoon salt
½ teaspoon Creole seasoning
½ cup Italian bread crumbs
Flour
2 tablespoons of olive oil

## Yield: 6–8 servings

- Pour the Unrivaled Red Sauce into a large heavy pot.

- Bring to a simmer over medium heat and stir.

- Place all the remaining meatball ingredients (except flour and olive oil) in mixing bowl. Stir well.

- Using your hands, shape meat to form meatballs.

- Roll lightly in flour.

- Heat the olive oil in a skillet over medium-high heat and cook the meatballs until lightly browned on all sides.

- Carefully place the meatballs into the sauce one by one.

- Simmer, uncovered, for 10 minutes before stirring. When the meatballs rise to the top, it's okay to stir.

- Stir the sauce and meatballs. Simmer for an additional 20 minutes and stir occasionally.

- Remove the sauce from the heat and serve over cooked pasta.

## Kid Notes

» Remember your egg-cracking skills (see Kid Notes on page 63).

» You can measure out and pour in all the ingredients that go into the bowl with the meat.

» Use your hands to thoroughly mix the meat and the seasoning, then roll it into balls, a little bit smaller than a ping pong ball.

» Put the flour in a shallow bowl and roll the meatballs around the flour to coat all sides.

» Ask for help when placing the meatballs in the hot olive oil, and then again into the hot Unrivaled Red Sauce.

» Remember to wash your hands after handling raw meat.

# Favorite Fettuccine Alfredo

## Kid Notes

» Ask an adult to help you drain the cooked pasta.

» Keep potholders handy.

» Make sure that the cream comes just to a boil, and then turn down the heat.

» Use as much Parmesan cheese as you like. Enjoy your pasta dish!

*6 quarts water*
*1 tablespoon salt*
*1 pound fettuccine pasta*
*2 cups heavy cream*
*2 cups Parmesan cheese, grated, plus more for*
*    sprinkling on top*
*Salt and pepper, to taste*
*Pinch of ground nutmeg*

### Yield: 6 servings

- Pour the water into a large pot and add 1 tablespoon salt. Set the pot over high heat, cover with the lid, and bring the water to a boil. Remove the lid. Slowly and carefully add the pasta, and then stir it with a long-handled fork. Boil the pasta, uncovered, until al dente (tender, but still firm to the bite), about 9 minutes, or according to package directions. Stir occasionally to prevent from sticking.

- While the pasta is boiling, pour the cream into a medium saucepan and add salt, pepper, and nutmeg. Set the pan over high heat and bring the cream to a boil. Reduce the heat to medium, stirring occasionally with a wooden spoon until slightly thickened, about 5 minutes. Remove the pan from the heat and set aside until the pasta is ready.

- Set the colander in the sink. Have the potholders ready. When the pasta is cooked, pour the contents of the pot into the colander. Drain quickly, shaking the colander, and dump the pasta back into the pot.

- Add the warm cream to the pasta. Add the Parmesan cheese. Using 2 wooden spoons, toss until the ingredients are well blended. Allow about 2 minutes for the pasta to absorb some of the sauce.

- Spoon the pasta onto plates. Serve immediately. Sprinkle top with grated cheese.

# Caesar Salad with Homemade Croutons

## Croutons:
1 cup olive oil
½ cup Parmesan cheese, freshly grated
2 tablespoons garlic, minced
1 teaspoon fresh oregano, chopped
1 teaspoon fresh thyme, chopped
1 pound day-old bread, preferably sourdough, sliced
    and cut into 1-inch cubes (about 4 cups)

## Caesar Vinaigrette:
1 egg
4 tablespoons fresh lemon juice
1 tablespoon garlic, minced
1 teaspoon Worcestershire sauce
¼ teaspoon red pepper flakes
1 tablespoon Dijon mustard
2 teaspoons anchovy paste
¾ cup peanut oil
¼ cup extra-virgin olive oil
¼ cup Parmesan cheese, freshly grated
Kosher salt and freshly ground black pepper

## Salad:
3 heads baby romaine lettuce, or 1 large head
    romaine lettuce, washed and patted dry
Parmesan cheese, freshly grated (optional)

Yield: 8–10 servings of salad; 2 cups of vinaigrette.
  Any leftover vinaigrette will keep in a covered
  container in the refrigerator for three days.

## Kid Notes

» The croutons can be made 4–5 days ahead of time and stored in a Ziploc bag. You will use 6 cloves of garlic in this recipe.

» You will need to press three cloves of garlic for the vinaigrette dressing.

» Remember when measuring liquid ingredients, such as the olive oil and the peanut oil, to use a liquid measuring cup.

## To Make Croutons:

- Preheat oven to 350°.

- In a medium bowl, combine the oil, cheese, garlic, oregano, and thyme. Add the bread and toss, coating all the croutons.

- Arrange the croutons in a single layer on a baking tray and bake until golden, turning to brown on all sides, about 15–20 minutes. Cool and store in a cool, dry place.

## To Prepare Caesar Vinaigrette:

- Crack the egg.

- In a medium bowl, whisk together the egg, lemon juice, garlic, Worcestershire sauce, red pepper flakes, mustard, and anchovy paste.

- While continuing to whisk, add the oils in a slow, steady stream until the dressing is thoroughly combined.

- Stir in the cheese and season with salt and pepper. Refrigerate in a covered container. When ready to use, whisk again.

## To Assemble Salad:

- Tear the lettuce into bite-sized pieces and place in a large salad bowl.

- Toss with enough Caesar Vinaigrette dressing to lightly coat.

- Arrange on salad plates and sprinkle with croutons and a little Parmesan cheese, if desired.

# Crusty Italian Bread

1 package rapid-rise dry yeast
1 tablespoon sugar
1 cup warm water (105°–115°)
2½ cups bread flour
1½ teaspoons salt
1 teaspoon balsamic vinegar
¼ cup extra-virgin olive oil with 1 teaspoon salt, warmed
Cornmeal (enough to sprinkle in loaf pans, about 2 tablespoons)

Yield: 2 loaves

- Preheat oven to 425°.

- Dissolve yeast and sugar in warm water until bubbly, 5–10 minutes.

- Place flour and salt in food processor with metal blade in place and pulse to mix. Add dissolved yeast and vinegar. Process 15–20 seconds.

- Turn dough out onto an unfloured, lightly oiled board and hand-knead a few times by pressing and folding the dough, using the heel of your hand.

- Place dough in a warm, oiled bowl and turn to coat. Cover and allow to rise until doubled, 45 minutes to an hour. Punch dough down, cut into halves, and form each half into a cylinder.

- Place the halves in 2 greased French bread pans that have been lightly sprinkled with cornmeal. Glaze with warm, salted oil. Allow to rise until doubled again, 30–45 minutes.

- Bake 15–20 minutes, or until golden brown and crusty.

- Serve with lots of butter.

## Kid Notes

» It is fun and easy to make bread at home.

» The warm water that you add to the yeast should feel like a baby's bath water—not too hot, but just right.

» When the yeast is bubbly, it is ready to be added to the flour and salt. Add the vinegar and push the "on" button on the food processor. Let it run for about 20 seconds.

» While the dough is rising, you can work on the other dishes to be served.

Note: After the dough is shaped into cylinders, you may freeze the loaves by covering them with plastic wrap and placing in a Ziploc bag. The dough may be frozen up to a month.

# Totally Terrific Tiramisu

2 ounces dark chocolate
1 cup mascarpone cheese
8 ounces cream cheese, softened
2 cups sour cream
½ cup sugar
1½ cups brewed decaf coffee (regular works too!)
20 lady fingers

## Yield: 6–8 servings

- Finely grate the chocolate with a grater or food processor.

- Combine the mascarpone, sour cream, cream cheese, and sugar in a large bowl and whisk until smooth and thoroughly combined.

- Pour the coffee into a shallow dish. Pull the lady fingers apart. Dip each lady finger lightly into coffee.

- Place lady fingers along the sides of a 2-quart glass dish, then cover the bottom with lady fingers, (round side down), making sure they fit snugly.

- Cover the lady fingers with a layer of cheese mixture and sprinkle with a little of the grated chocolate.

- Repeat the layers, finishing with cheese mixture. Sprinkle this with remaining chocolate and chill in the refrigerator for 2–3 hours.

# south of the border

Just the words "We're having Mexican food!" make supper time a fiesta. When Leslie was growing up, this was a festive favorite pre-game supper for the cheerleaders. Our families and friends are still cheering for this sensational South-of-the-Border supper that can and should be started the day before. Chicken breasts for enchiladas and the ground beef for tacos can be cooked and seasoned beforehand. And there are plenty of tasks for kids of all ages. They delight in grating cheese and are adept at filling and rolling the enchiladas. The nacho breadsticks use lots of fine motor skills. Mango salsa is an "at home café" invention by Leslie and her kids and has become a family favorite. The Mexican chocolate cake is a "no mess" one-dish wonder.

Sour Cream Eat Ya Enchiladas

Fiesta Rice

Tempting Taco Quesadillas

Mostly Mango Salsa

Nothing to It Nacho Breadsticks

Mexican Made-in-the-Pan Chocolate Cake

# Sour Cream Eat Ya Enchiladas

*6 boneless, skinless chicken breasts*
*Extra-virgin olive oil*
*Creole seasoning*
*2 tablespoons butter*
*4 tablespoons onion, chopped*
*One 4.5-ounce can chopped green chiles*
*8 ounces cream cheese*
*8 ounces sour cream*
*1 12-count package flour tortillas*
*12 ounces cheddar cheese, grated*
*12 ounces pepper jack cheese, grated*
*1 cup salsa*

### Yield: 6 servings

- Preheat oven to 350°.

- Coat chicken with olive oil and Creole seasoning.

- Place in baking dish and bake at until tender, about 25 minutes. Cool and cut into cubes.

- Spray 9- by 13-inch (3-quart) glass baking dish with nonstick cooking spray.

- In a saucepan, melt butter. Add onion and sauté until clear.

- Add green chilies, sour cream, and cream cheese, stirring constantly until smooth and well blended. Mix in cubed chicken.

- Spoon 2–3 tablespoons of the mixture down the center of each tortilla.

- Top each tortilla evenly with cheese and salsa.

- Fold one side over filling; then roll and place seam side down in prepared baking dish.

- Spoon the remaining cheese and salsa over the filled tortillas. Cover with foil.

- Bake for 25–30 minutes, or until hot and bubbly.

- Remove foil and return to oven; bake uncovered an additional 5 minutes.

## Kid Notes

» Be sure and wash your hands after handling the raw chicken. Have an adult help you put the chicken in the oven and take it out of the oven.

» The chicken will cut easily with a table knife; however the onion may call for a sharper knife. Ask for a little help.

## Kid Notes

» Chopping the onion will be the hardest thing to do for this recipe. Ask for help whenever you use a sharp knife.

» You will also need an adult to assist you with sautéing the vegetables and rice and putting the dish in the oven and taking it out.

# Fiesta Rice

*4 tablespoons olive oil*
*1 large onion, finely chopped*
*1½ cups medium-grained rice, uncooked*
*2 cloves garlic, minced, or 1 teaspoon garlic powder*
*4 cups water*
*2 8-ounce cans tomato sauce*
*1 tablespoon chili powder*
*1 teaspoon salt*
*½ teaspoon pepper*
*1 cup cheddar cheese, grated*
*2 cups Monterey Jack cheese, grated*

**Yield: 6–8 servings.**

- Preheat oven to 450°.
- In a medium saucepan, sauté onions and garlic in olive oil until tender.
- Add rice and continue to cook until golden color.
- Add water, tomato sauce, and seasonings. Cover and simmer for 20–25 minutes.
- Spray 2-quart casserole with cooking spray or grease with butter.
- Spoon rice mixture into casserole and top with cheese.
- Bake 5–8 minutes or until cheese bubbles.

# Tempting Taco Quesadillas

*1 pound ground beef*
*¾ cup water*
*1 package taco seasoning*
*2 avocados, peeled and sliced (optional)*
*8 ounces cheddar cheese, finely shredded*
*1 package soft flour tortillas*
*Taco sauce*

## Yield: 6 servings

- Brown the meat in a skillet over medium-high heat, stirring to break up any lumps. Carefully drain and discard any excess oil.

- Add the taco seasoning and water to the beef and stir to combine. Bring the mixture to a boil. Reduce heat to a simmer and cook, uncovered, stirring occasionally, for 10 minutes.

- Preheat oven to 425° and spray a baking sheet with nonstick cooking spray.

- Spoon some of the meat mixture over half of each tortilla.

- Top with avocados and cheese.

- Drizzle with taco sauce.

- Fold tortillas in half and, using a metal spatula, transfer to the prepared baking sheet.

- Bake for 15–20 minutes or until heated through and cheese is melted.

## Kid Notes

» You will need help browning the meat and draining it, too.

» When assembling the quesadillas, you can put as much meat, cheese, or other ingredients on the tortilla as you prefer just as long as the tortilla folds over.

# Mostly Mango Salsa

*2 large mangoes, peeled and chopped*
*8 tomatillos, finely chopped*
*1 orange or yellow bell pepper, cored, seeded, and finely chopped*
*½ cup cilantro, finely chopped*
*½ cup red onion, finely chopped*
*¼ teaspoon salt*
*1 teaspoon ground cumin*
*Juice from 1 lime*

### Yield: 3 cups

- Place all ingredients in a medium-sized bowl and stir until thoroughly combined.

- Add more salt and lime juice as desired.

# Nothing to It Nacho Breadsticks

*¾ cup spicy nacho-flavored tortilla chips (about 30 chips), finely crushed*
*1 11-ounce can refrigerated breadsticks*

**Yield: 12 breadsticks**

- Preheat oven to 375°.

- Crush tortilla chips by placing in a Ziploc bag and crumbling with your hands until finely crushed.

- Place crushed tortilla chips in shallow dish or pan.

- Separate breadstick dough into strips.

- Roll both sides of each piece of dough in the tortilla chips, pressing to adhere slightly.

- Twist each strip twice. Place the strips on a large, ungreased cookie sheet, pressing ends down firmly.

- Bake for 13–15 minutes, or until golden brown. Serve warm.

## Kid Notes

» Place the tortillas chips in a Ziploc bag and crush with your fingers.

» The crushed chips will stick to the breadstick dough.

» Ask for help when placing the pan in and removing it from the oven.

# Mexican Made-in-the-Pan Chocolate Cake

1¼ cups all-purpose flour
⅓ cup unsweetened cocoa
1 cup sugar
½ teaspoon salt
¾ teaspoon baking soda

½ teaspoon cinnamon
1 cup water
⅓ cup canola or vegetable oil
1 teaspoon vanilla extract
1 teaspoon cider vinegar or white vinegar

**Yield: 8 servings**

- Preheat oven to 325°.

- Lightly grease an 8-inch square cake pan.

- Sift flour, cocoa, sugar, salt, baking soda, and cinnamon into square pan.

- Mix it slowly, taking turns with a fork and a soup spoon, until it is completely light brown.

- When the dry ingredients are all mixed, make 4 dents with a spoon—2 large and 2 small—in the mixture.

- Pour water into one of the large dents.

- Pour oil into the other large dent.

- Pour vanilla extract into one of the small dents.

- Pour vinegar into the other small dent.

- Begin stirring slowly with a fork in little circles to get all of the dry parts wet.

- As it turns into batter, start mashing it down with a fork. After you mash a few times, scrape the bottom and stir. Do this again many times: mash, scrape, and stir.

- When the batter is smooth, scrape the sides one more time with a rubber spatula and spread the batter into place.

- Bake for 30 minutes.

- Cool the cake in the pan for 30 minutes before cutting it into squares.

## Kid Notes

» This is the easiest cake in the world to make! Just follow the directions given.

» Ask for help when placing the pan in and removing it from the oven.

# unfancy french

Vive la France! The children in our cooking classes love to learn about France while making this menu. We talk about the Eiffel Tower, the Louvre, the fields of lavender, and the special emphasis the French people place on food while flipping crêpes and beating egg whites. The children enjoy the exotic menu and surprise their parents by enthusiastically eating foods not normally found on the family table. It's been our experience that the way to get kids to eat green beans (and other vegetables) is to let them do the cooking. Kids love to snap the green beans in this class and always come back for seconds.

Bistro Brown Sugar Glazed Brie

Chicken & Mushroom Crêpes

Freshest French Green Beans (Haricot Verts)

Fabulous French Dressing
on Mixed Baby Greens

Paris Popovers

Your Very Own Chocolate Soufflé
with Vanilla Ice Cream

# Bistro Brown Sugar Glazed Brie

*1 pound wheel of brie, rind removed*
*1 cup pecans, chopped (optional)*
*2 cups light brown sugar*
*¼ cup butter, melted*
*crackers*

## Yield: 8 servings

- Preheat oven to 300°.

- Place brie on a pie plate.

- Mix brown sugar and pecans, place on top of brie and drizzle with butter.

- Place in oven and heat for 8–10 minutes until brie melts.

- Serve immediately with crackers.

## Kid Notes

» The rind is the firm outer layer of the cheese. It cuts easily with a knife.

» It is easy to melt the butter in the microwave— about 30–40 seconds for ¼ cup.

» Ask for help when placing the brie in and removing it from the oven.

## Kid Notes

» Sauté is a French word which means to cook in a small amount of hot butter or oil in a shallow pan, stirring often until ready. You will need adult assistance when cooking on the stove.

» Whisking helps to remove any lumps from the cream sauce.

» The crêpes are thin but not so dainty that you should be worried about tearing them when you roll the chicken mixture inside.

» Ask for help when placing the pan in and removing it from the oven.

» Wipe mushrooms clean using a paper towel. Slice using a plastic or table knife.

# Chicken & Mushroom Crêpes

*12 Crêpes!!! (see page 102)*
*5 ounces fresh mushrooms, sliced*
*3 tablespoons butter, melted*
*⅓ cup flour*
*1¼ cups chicken broth, reserved from cooking chicken*
*¾ cup heavy cream*
*⅓ cup dry cooking sherry*
*4 ounces white cheddar cheese, grated*
*1 pound chicken, cooked and chopped (2 cups)*
*4 tablespoons Parmesan cheese, grated*

### Yield: 12 crêpes

- Gently boil chicken in 4 quarts of water and 1 tablespoon of salt until cooked. When chicken is cool, cut into bite-sized pieces. Reserve 1¼ cups of broth.

- Sauté mushrooms in butter until soft.

- Add flour, broth, cream, sherry, and white cheddar cheese, stirring well after each.

- Blend until smooth.

- Add 1 cup of cream sauce to chicken.

- Place 3 tablespoons chicken mixture in each crepe, roll up, and place in buttered casserole dish.

- Pour remaining sauce over crêpes and sprinkle with Parmesan cheese.

- Bake at 375° for 20 minutes.

# Crêpes!!!

*3 large eggs*
*1½ cups milk*
*1 cup plus 2 tablespoons all-purpose flour*
*1 teaspoon sugar (1 tablespoon for dessert crêpes)*
*2 tablespoons butter, melted*

## Yield: 12 crêpes

- Put all ingredients in a blender in the order listed and blend them until the batter is smooth.

- Remove the lid and scrape down the sides with a rubber spatula.

- Briefly blend the mixture again.

- Set the covered blender in the refrigerator for at least 30 minutes or up to 2 days.

- When ready to cook the crêpes, use a paper towel to spread about 1 teaspoon of butter or vegetable oil in the bottom of an 8- or 9-inch nonstick skillet with low sides or a crêpe pan. Heat the skillet on a stove top burner set at medium. Blend the batter again to smooth it.

- For the first crêpe, pour one fourth to one third cup of batter into measuring cup to help gauge how much to use.

- Cook each crêpe, following the steps below. Adjust the heat if they brown too quickly or too slowly.

- Pour the batter into your heated pan. Immediately tilt and swirl the pan to evenly coat the bottom. This should take about 5 seconds.

- Cook the crêpe on the first side for about 45 seconds, then quickly flip it with a spatula and cook the other side for about half as long.

- Grasping the pan securely, swiftly invert it so the cooked crêpe will fall onto a large plate. Wipe the skillet with a paper towel and rub a little butter in the pan before cooking the next crêpe.

## Kid Notes

» A crêpe is a thin pancake. It can be filled with something sweet or savory.

» The cooked crêpes can be layered between wax paper, wrapped airtight, and frozen for up to 1 month.

» Crack the eggs in a separate bowl (see Kid Notes on page 63) before pouring into the blender.

## Kid Notes

» Snapping the beans means to remove the tops and tails from the beans. Remove the string, if there is one.

» Boiling the beans gives them a bright color and a plump texture.

» These beans can be cooked in the microwave. Place in a 1-quart microwave-safe dish and add 1 tablespoon water and 1 teaspoon salt. Cover with plastic wrap and cook on high for about 8 minutes. Let stand for 2 minutes. Then add the cream, butter, salt, and pepper, and stir.

# Freshest French Green Beans (Haricot Verts)

*1 pound fresh green beans*
*5 cups cold water*
*1 teaspoon salt*
*1 tablespoon butter*
*Salt and pepper, to taste*
*¼ cup heavy cream*

**Yield: 6 servings**

- Place the green beans in a colander and wash them under cool running water in the sink.

- Snap off both ends of the beans with your fingers.

- Put the water and 1 teaspoon salt into a medium saucepan. Bring to a rapid boil over medium-high heat.

- Using tongs, carefully add the beans to the boiling water. Cover the saucepan and simmer the beans on medium-low heat for 10 minutes, or until crisp-tender.

- Place the colander in the sink and pour the beans and water into the colander. After the water has drained off, put the beans back into the saucepan.

- Add the butter to the saucepan and sprinkle with salt and pepper to taste. Add the cream and stir gently to coat the beans well.

- Spoon the beans into a bowl and serve.

# Fabulous French Dressing on Mixed Baby Greens

*2 12-ounce bags mixed baby salad greens*
*1 cup walnuts, toasted and chopped*
*½ cup red onion, thinly sliced*
*1 avocado, thinly sliced*
*Fabulous French Dressing*

## Yield: 6–8 servings

- On a baking sheet, place walnuts in a 400° oven for about 10 minutes, until toasted.

- Place salad greens, onion, and avocado in a salad bowl.

- Toss lightly with Fabulous French Dressing.

- Sprinkle toasted walnuts on top. Serve.

# Fabulous French Dressing

*8 ounces garlic vinegar*
*2 teaspoons salt*
*1 teaspoon Tabasco sauce*
*⅛ teaspoon red pepper (nearly cover surface)*
*1 teaspoon garlic powder*
*¼ teaspoon paprika*
*3 heaping teaspoons Dijon mustard*
*16 ounces (½ liter) olive oil*

Yield: 3 cups

- In a quart mason jar, mix the vinegar, salt, Tabasco, red pepper, garlic powder, and paprika together. Cover jar and shake well.

- Open jar and add Dijon to the vinegar mixture. Cover jar and shake well.

- Finally, open jar and add the olive oil. Re-cover jar and shake until olive oil and vinegar mixture are well combined.

## Kid Notes

» Feel free to add any of your favorite vegetables to this salad.

» When shaking salad dressing, make sure the lid to the jar is on tight.

» Add dressing a little bit at a time—coat the vegetables lightly. You can always add more!

# Paris Popovers

*3 cups milk*
*3 ¾ cups all-purpose flour*
*1½ teaspoons salt*
*1 teaspoon baking powder*
*6 large eggs, room temperature*

**Yield: 12 popovers**

- Preheat oven to 450°.

- Place milk in glass measuring cup and microwave for 1 minute or until warm to touch.

- Sift flour, salt, and baking powder into a large mixing bowl.

- Crack eggs into a mixing bowl and beat at medium speed for about 3 minutes until pale in color.

- With mixer on low speed, gradually add flour mixture and milk; then beat on medium speed for 2 minutes.

- Allow batter to rest for about 30 minutes at room temperature.

- Spray popover pan with cooking spray and fill cups with batter until almost to the top.

- Place popover pan on a baking sheet and bake for 15 minutes.

- Turn down the temperature to 375° without opening oven and bake for 30 minutes or longer until golden brown.

- Serve warm.

## Kid Notes

» Crack eggs into a separate bowl before adding to the mixing bowl (see Kid Notes on page 63).

» Sift all of the lumps out of the flour, baking powder, and salt mixture.

» You can use a hand mixer or a standing mixer.

» Set the timer for 15 minutes when an adult puts the pan in the oven. When it beeps, don't peek but do turn the oven to 375°. Set the timer for 30 more minutes, then clean up your room or set the table until the popovers are ready!

# Your Very Own Chocolate Soufflé with Vanilla Ice Cream

*¼ cup butter*
*½ cup sugar*
*1 cup semisweet chocolate chips*
*3 tablespoons heavy cream*
*1 tablespoon flour*
*1 tablespoon vanilla extract*
*8 eggs, room temperature*
*2 scoops vanilla ice cream, softened*

## Yield: 8 servings

- For this recipe you will need eight 3-inch ramekins or ovenproof bowls.

- Preheat oven to 375°.

- Grease each ramekin with butter. Sprinkle in 1 teaspoon of sugar.

- Rotate the ramekin to coat the inside and then pour out the excess sugar.

- Combine the chocolate chips, heavy cream, flour, and vanilla extract in a double boiler and stir the mixture over low heat until melted and smooth.

- Keep the mixture warm until you are ready to use it by leaving it over hot water, not on the burner.

- Separate the eggs, placing the whites in one bowl.

- Whisk yolks.

- When they are blended, gradually whisk in several

## Kid Notes

» Separate the eggs and make sure the whites are placed into a clean mixing bowl (See Kid Notes page 61.)

» Use a paper towel with about 1 teaspoon of butter on it to grease the ramekins. Just rub the bottom and sides with the buttered paper towel.

» A double boiler is used to cook foods that scorch easily and cannot hold up to direct heat. You can make your own double boiler if you do not own one. Put about 1 inch of water in a saucepan and rest a heat-resistant bowl that fits snugly into the saucepan, leaving 2–3 inches between the bottom of the bowl and the saucepan. Heat on stove top until melted

tablespoons of the melted chocolate mixture. Add slowly so it does not cook the eggs.

- Repeat until half of the chocolate has been added, then whisk in the remaining chocolate at once.

- Using an electric mixer, beat the egg whites until stiff peaks form.

- Using a rubber spatula, gently fold a fourth of the beaten egg whites into the chocolate mixture until just combined.

- Continue folding in the remaining egg whites until well blended.

- Working quickly but carefully, divide the mixture among the ramekins, filling each to ½ inch from the top.

- Bake the soufflés on a sheet pan in the center of the oven until well puffed, about 12–15 minutes.

- Remove the soufflés from the oven.

- Using a spoon, carefully make a small slit in the top of each soufflé and fill with some softened vanilla ice cream.

- Careful—the ramekins are very hot! Enjoy!

# it's greek to me!

Every time a child is christened in Leslie's family, out comes Mom's Marvelous Chicken Phyllo. Our Greek themed cooking classes are always a hit! The children love the different tastes and enjoy working with phyllo. Phyllo pastry seems a little intimidating to adults and kids alike, but after doing it once, you realize that there is nothing to it! In our classes, young cooks never tire of making our Big Fat Greek Pizza. The crust for this unique "pizza" is made by layering sheets of phyllo in a baking pan and topping it with layers of yummy ingredients. All of these are very "hands on" recipes. The mix and match menu features a salad and a variety of main courses from which to choose.

Big Fat Greek Pizza

Pastitsio with Pizzazz!

Mom's Marvelous Chicken Phyllo

Tossed Greek Salad Bowl

Feta Pita Toast

The Very Best Baklava

# Big Fat Greek Pizza

1 package phyllo pastry dough
½ cup butter, melted
¼ cup olive oil
2 tablespoons olive oil
1 cup onions, finely chopped
¼ teaspoon salt
3 large cloves garlic, crushed
½ teaspoon dried basil, crushed
½ teaspoon dried oregano
Juice from ½ large lemon
1 pound fresh spinach, cleaned, stemmed, and
    chopped, or 1 10-ounce package frozen,
    chopped spinach
1 pound mozzarella cheese, grated
1½ cups crumbled feta or farmer's cheese
4 roma tomatoes, in thin slices
¾ cup fine bread crumbs
Freshly ground black pepper, to taste

Yield: 8 servings

## Kid Notes

» Rub the butter on a large baking tray by smoothing about 1 tablespoon all over with your fingertips. You can also use a paper towel.

» Use a garlic press to crush the garlic. Ask for help when using a sharp knife to chop the onion.

» Have an adult help you with sautéing the vegetables on the stove top.

» Lightly "paint" each sheet of phyllo with the butter/olive oil mixture using a pastry brush. This will be your Greek pizza crust.

» Place the thawed spinach in a colander in the sink and squeeze into a ball with paper towels to remove the moisture.

» Spoon on the spinach (it's good!) and arrange the other toppings.

» Ask for help when placing the pizza in and removing it from the oven.

- Preheat oven to 400°. Butter a large baking tray. Also, combine melted butter with ¼ cup olive oil. Set aside.

- In a large skillet, cook the onions and garlic with salt in 2 tablespoons olive oil, until the onions are clear and soft. Add herbs, lemon juice, and spinach, and cook over fairly high heat, stirring until the spinach is limp and the liquid is evaporated.

- On the buttered baking tray begin layering the sheets of phyllo dough, brushing each surface with a generous amount of combined butter and olive oil. Continue layering the pastry sheets until you have used them all. Brush the top surface of the stack with the remaining butter/olive oil mixture.

- Use a slotted spoon to transfer the spinach mixture from the skillet to the pastry stack, leaving behind whatever liquid failed to evaporate. Spread the spinach mixture evenly in place, leaving a ½-inch border of pastry.

- Sprinkle on the crumbled feta or farmer's cheese, plus half the mozzarella.

- Dredge the tomato slices in bread crumbs, arrange these on top of the pizza, and toss the remaining mozzarella over the tomatoes.

- Bake uncovered for 20–25 minutes.

# Pastitsio with Pizzazz!

1 tablespoon olive oil
1 medium onion, finely chopped
2 garlic cloves, pressed
1 pound lean ground beef
2 14.5-ounce cans diced tomatoes, drained
2 teaspoons dried oregano
1½ teaspoons cinnamon
1¾ teaspoons salt, divided
¼ teaspoon freshly ground pepper
8 ounces elbow macaroni
3 tablespoons butter
⅓ cup all-purpose flour
1 quart whole milk
2 large eggs
1 cup Parmesan cheese, freshly grated, divided
1 cup feta cheese, crumbled

### Yield: 8 servings

- Preheat oven to 375°.

- Heat oil in a large skillet over medium heat. Add the onion and garlic and cook, stirring occasionally, until onion is translucent, 7 minutes.

- Stir in beef and cook, breaking up meat with the back of a spoon, until browned, about 7 minutes. Spoon off all but 1 tablespoon of fat.

- Stir in tomatoes, oregano, cinnamon, 1 teaspoon salt, and pepper.

- Bring to a boil, then reduce heat to low, cover and simmer, 15 minutes. Uncover and simmer 15 minutes more.

- Meanwhile, cook macaroni according to package directions. Drain.

- Melt butter in a large saucepan over medium heat. Whisk in flour for 1 minute.

- Increase heat to high. Whisking constantly add the milk and remaining salt. Bring to a boil and remove from heat.

## Kid Notes

» Ask for help when using a sharp knife to chop the onion. Use a garlic press to crush the garlic.

» You will need an adult to help you cook on the stove top, drain the macaroni and make the white sauce.

» Crack the eggs in a separate bowl (see Kid Notes on page 63) and beat with a whisk or a fork.

» Ask for help when placing the pastitsio in and removing it from the oven. Serve proudly!

- In a small bowl, beat eggs using a whisk. Beat 1 cup of the hot cream-sauce mixture into the eggs, then beat the egg mixture into the cream sauce. Whisk in ¾ cup Parmesan cheese.

- Grease a shallow, 9- by 13-inch baking dish.

- Transfer half of the macaroni to prepared dish. Layer with 1½ cups of the cheese sauce. Spread the beef mixture evenly over cheese sauce. Layer with the remaining macaroni, then sprinkle with feta cheese. Top with remaining cheese sauce and sprinkle with remaining Parmesan cheese.

- Bake in a 375° oven until golden and bubbling, 35 minutes. Let stand until firm.

# Mom's Marvelous Chicken Phyllo

*6 cups cooked chicken breast, cut into bite-sized pieces*
*3 cups thick white sauce (ingredients below)*
*8 ounces cream cheese, softened*
*1 bunch green onions (tops and all), chopped*
*1 cup celery, chopped*
*Salt and pepper, to taste*
*1 teaspoon seafood seasoning*
*¼ cup dry cooking sherry*
*1 package phyllo pastry dough*
*½ cup butter, melted*

## White Sauce:

*¾ cup butter*
*¾ cup flour*
*1½ cups milk*
*1½ cups chicken broth*
*Salt and pepper, to taste*

**Yield: 8 servings**

- Preheat oven to 350°.

- Grease a 9- by 13-inch casserole dish.

- Gently boil chicken breast in stockpot filled with water. Season water with salt and pepper. Allow chicken breast to cool and cut into bite-sized pieces. Save 1½ cups chicken broth for the white sauce.

- Make white sauce by melting ¾ cup of butter in a large saucepan. Add flour and stir with a whisk until thickened. Slowly add milk and chicken broth, constantly stirring with whisk until completely blended. Cook over medium heat until a thick sauce is made.

- Add softened cream cheese to the white sauce. Stir in the vegetables. Blend well.

- Mix salt, pepper, seafood seasoning, and sherry.

- Place in casserole dish.

- Layer one sheet of phyllo dough on top of the chicken mixture in the casserole dish. Brush generously with butter, then add another sheet. Repeat until there are 11 layers.

- Bake for 40–45 minutes until top is light brown and the filling is bubbly.

- Allow to set for 5–10 minutes before serving.

## Kid Notes

» Place chicken breast on a cutting board.

» Use a plastic or table knife to cut the chicken.

» Ask for help when using the stove top to cook the white sauce.

» Use a pastry brush to "paint" the butter on each pastry sheet.

» Ask for help when placing the chicken phyllo in and removing it from the oven.

» This is so creamy and yummy!

# Tossed Greek Salad Bowl

## Kid Notes

» Wash lettuce by rinsing in a colander in the sink. Pat dry on paper towels.

» Measure the dressing ingredients into a bowl and whisk until blended together.

» Layer the ingredients in a bowl in the order given—the colors will look good enough to eat!

## Salad:

1 head romaine lettuce, washed, dried, and torn into bite-sized pieces
½ head iceberg lettuce, washed, dried, and torn into bite-sized pieces
12 cherry tomatoes
1 cup feta, crumbled
½ small red onion, chopped
1 cucumber, peeled and chopped, seeds removed
12 kalamata olives, pitted and cut in half
6 pepperoncini peppers

## Dressing:

6 tablespoons olive oil
4 tablespoons fresh lemon juice
2 teaspoons garlic, minced
1 teaspoon dried oregano
1 2-ounce can anchovies, mashed
½ teaspoon salt, or to taste
½ teaspoon pepper, or to taste
½ teaspoon sugar

Yield: 8 servings

- In a large bowl, layer the salad ingredients in the order given.

- Place the dressing ingredients into a blender and pulse until combined.

- When ready to serve salad, pour the dressing over layered ingredients and toss.

# Feta Pita Toast

*2 tablespoons butter*
*½ cup onion, chopped*
*8 ounces feta cheese, crumbled*
*1 teaspoon lemon juice*
*½ teaspoon Greek seasoning*
*Pinch cayenne pepper*
*1 package pita bread*
*½ cup Parmesan cheese, grated*

## Yield: 8 servings

- Melt butter in a medium skillet. Add chopped onion and sauté for 2–3 minutes over medium heat.

- Remove from heat and add the feta, lemon juice, Greek seasoning, and cayenne.

- Preheat oven to 400°.

- Line baking sheet with parchment paper.

- Cut pita bread in half, and the halves in half to make four wedges. Then make the four wedges into eight wedges by cutting apart.

- Place 1 heaping tablespoon of feta mixture on each pita wedge then place on a baking sheet.

- Sprinkle with Parmesan.

- Bake for 10–12 minutes, until the cheeses are slightly melted and hot. Serve.

## Kid Notes

» Ask for assistance sautéing ingredients on the stove top.

» Cut the pita bread into triangles. It is like cutting a pie. You can do this with a table knife.

» Have an adult help you place the baking pan in and take it out of the oven.

# The Very Best Baklava

*1 package phyllo pastry, thawed*
*½ cup butter, melted*

## Filling for Baklava:

*¾ cup light brown sugar*
*½ teaspoon cinnamon*
*¼ teaspoon allspice*
*¼ cup butter, melted*
*2 cups pecans or walnuts, finely chopped*

Yield: About 3 dozen

- Preheat oven to 350°.

- Make filling by mixing the ingredients with a fork in a medium bowl. Set aside.

- Keep phyllo covered with a slightly damp towel and work with one sheet at a time.

- Place one sheet of phyllo on the work surface and brush entire sheet with butter. Repeat until you have six layers

- Cut buttered sheet into strips (2 inches by 14 inches).

- Place a heaping teaspoon of filling on one end of a strip.

- Fold the bottom left corner over to right side. Then fold the bottom right corner over to the left side. Continue folding flag-fashion until the entire strip is folded into a triangle shape. Repeat the above steps using the remaining sheets of phyllo.

- Again, brush the flags with butter.

- Place on baking sheet. Bake for 15–20 minutes or until golden brown.

## Kid Notes

» You can chop the pecans or walnuts in a food processor by using short pulses.

» Scissors work great when cutting the phyllo dough into strips.

» "Paint" butter on the strips using a pastry brush.

» This is just like folding an American flag!

» Ask for help when placing the baklava in and removing it from the oven.

# sleep over party!

A sleep over party conjures up visions of late night fun and frivolity for kids, and this menu offers a creative alternative to the incessant chatter of television and drone of video games. This was our first cooking class menu, and it was such a hit that we have now taught close to a hundred classes. It is always a success with both kids and parents alike. Totally kid friendly, the parents are "wowed" by the cute, creative, and balanced food items the kids prepare. Get things started with the ever-requested "All Night Nacho Dip," and then let everyone decorate his or her own "Creatures in a Blanket." The Pajama Peanut Butter Balls are a no-cook treat that everyone will love, and then wash it all down with "Didn't Sleep a Wink Pink Drink." This funny food will captivate even the finickiest of eaters.

## Creatures in a Blanket
## Pajama Peanut Butter Balls
## All Night Nacho Dip
## No Curfew Caramel Popcorn
## Didn't Sleep A Wink Pink Drink

# Creatures in a Blanket

*2 8-ounce cans crescent dinner rolls*
*8 1-ounce slices cooked ham or turkey*
*8 single slices Swiss or cheddar cheese*
*16 frozen breaded wing-shaped chicken patties,*
  *slightly thawed*
*Squirt bottles of red ketchup, green or blue ketchup,*
  *and mustard*

## Yield: 8 servings

- Preheat oven to 375°.

- Line a sheet pan with parchment paper.

- Separate dough into eight 4- by 7½-inch rectangles and firmly press perforations to seal.

- For each sandwich, place one of the rectangles of dough on sheet pan.

- Top with 1 slice of ham or turkey at one end of the dough. Place 1 slice of cheese on top.

- Place 2 chicken patties, side by side, on ham or turkey and cheese.

- Fold ⅔ of dough over chicken from bottom up, leaving about 1½ inches of chicken uncovered, for the creatures' heads. Press sides of sandwich with fork to seal edges.

- Bake at 375° for 10–12 minutes, or until crust is golden brown and chicken is hot.

- Make faces and hair with ketchup and mustard. Mustard is great for the hair, green or blue ketchup is great for the eyes, and red ketchup is great for the mouth.

## Kid Notes

» We love using parchment paper for this. You can write the name of the person who made the "creatures" on the paper. That way once the sandwiches are cooked, they can decorate their own. Also, there is no messy, sticky clean up for the pan.

» There is a picture of this fun and yummy sandwich at the beginning of this chapter, if you need to "see" what you are doing.

» Ask for help placing the baking sheet in and removing it from the oven.

## Kid Notes

» You don't need to use an oven or stove for these—a "no cook" recipe.

» If the dough gets too sticky, roll in extra powdered sugar.

» Use the tips of your fingers to roll into balls instead of your whole hand. It is easier.

## Kid Notes

» This is going to be your most favorite dip!

» Just layer the ingredients, then microwave.

» You can add any of your favorite ingredients like black olives, jalapenos, green chilies, salsa, or green onions.

# Pajama Peanut Butter Balls

*1 cup peanut butter, creamy or crunchy*
*1 cup light corn syrup*
*1¼ cups powdered milk*
*1¼ cups powdered sugar*
*Extra powdered sugar for rolling*

**Yield: 24 peanut butter balls, depending on size**

- Place all ingredients in a mixing bowl and stir until thoroughly combined.

- Using your hands, roll mixture into as many small, bite-sized balls as possible.

- Place extra powdered sugar in a shallow pie tin or plate and roll balls in the sugar to coat.

- Eat and enjoy.

# All Night Nacho Dip

*2  8-ounce packages cream cheese*
*1  15-ounce can chili (no beans)*
*8 ounces Monterey Jack cheese, shredded, or a*
*    mixture of Monterey Jack and cheddar cheese.*
*Tortilla chips*

**Yield: About 3 cups**

- Using a spatula, spread the cream cheese in one layer along the bottom of your most festive 8- by 8-inch baking dish.

- Top with the chili and use a spoon to spread evenly over the cream cheese.

- Sprinkle the shredded cheese evenly over the chili.

- Microwave for about 4 minutes, or until melted.

- Enjoy with tortilla chips.

# No Curfew Caramel Popcorn

*1 cup sugar*
*½ cup butter*
*½ cup light corn syrup*
*1 teaspoon salt*
*1 teaspoon vanilla extract*
*½ teaspoon baking soda*
*2 3-ounce packages microwave popcorn, popped*
   *(16 cups)*

## Yield: 16 cups

- Preheat oven to 250°.

- Lightly grease 2 shallow roasting pans.

- In a saucepan, stir together the sugar, butter, light corn syrup, and salt.

- Bring to a boil over medium heat, stirring constantly.

- Remove mixture from heat, and stir in baking soda and vanilla extract.

- Place half of popcorn in each pan. Pour sugar mixture evenly over popcorn; stir well with a lightly greased spatula.

- Baked at 250° for 1 hour, stirring every 15 minutes. Spread on wax paper to cool, breaking apart large clumps as mixture cools.

- Store in airtight containers.

## Kid Notes

» You can pop the popcorn in the microwave!

» You will need help boiling the ingredients on the stove top and pouring the hot mixture on the popcorn.

» Use a long-handled wooden spoon to mix and stir.

# Didn't Sleep a Wink Pink Drink

*2 cups low-fat frozen vanilla yogurt*
*1 cup frozen sweetened strawberries, partially thawed*
*2 cups low-fat milk*
*8 cherries, for garnish*

## Yield: 8 servings

- Combine half the yogurt, half the strawberries, and half of the milk in a blender and whirl until smooth.

- Pour equal amounts into 4 glasses.

- Repeat steps 1, 2, and 3 with remaining yogurt, strawberries, and milk and pour into 4 more glasses.

- Add a cherry to each glass and serve.

Variation: Use your favorite fruit along with your favorite frozen yogurt to customize your smoothie.

Tip: If consistency of drink seems too thick to your taste, simply thin with a bit more milk. Use plastic fancy glasses to prevent breakage.

## Kid Notes

» Put all ingredients into the blender and push the blend button on and off until the ingredients are combined, and then blend well.

» You can pick your favorite fruit and yogurt using the same measurements.

# backyard burger bash

Backyard burgers are a traditional American family favorite. We've added a quirky ingredient, pickle juice, to moisten the ground chuck and add extra flavor, yet it almost seems an obvious choice. Making hamburger patties, peeling potatoes, and measuring for brownies are fun jobs for the younger kids, while slicing and grilling chores are reserved for older kids or adults. Rob, Leslie's teenaged son, is such an accomplished backyard cook that our Grilled Cheddar Burgers bear his name. Helen's niece, Katie, has been assisting in our cooking classes since she was twelve. When she heard we were looking for a recipe for Homemade Chips, she claimed that she had the BEST! And after trying Katie's Homemade Potato Chips, you'll agree. Fresh Peach Blueberry Cobbler is an incomparable summer treat and is easy to make with no crust required.

Rob's Grilled Cheddar Burgers

Katie's Homemade Potato Chips

Paint Magic

Slow Cooked BBQ Baked Beans

Backyard Brown Sugar Brownies

The Perfect Peach Blueberry Cobbler

# Rob's Grilled Cheddar Burgers

*2 pounds ground chuck, 20 percent fat is ideal*
*2 tablespoons dill pickle juice*
*2 tablespoons Montreal Steak Seasoning*
*8 hamburger buns*
*8 slices cheddar cheese*

**Yield: 8 large or 10 medium hamburger patties**

- In medium bowl, combine ground chuck, pickle juice, and steak seasoning; mix well.

- Make into patties of 1-inch thickness.

- Make sure the grill is good and hot.

- Grill over a hot fire, flipping once, for about 4–5 minutes per side for medium doneness. Add cheese after flipping.

- If you are not using a grill to cook the burgers, then heat a large nonstick skillet over medium-high heat until hot.

- Add patties; cook about 4–5 minutes per side, turning once.

- Remove patties from skillet; cover to keep warm.

- If desired, serve with ketchup, mustard, or chili sauce.

## Kid Notes

» Be sure to wash your hands before and after handling the hamburger meat.

» Use your hands to mix the meat and seasonings— it combines the ingredients well and it is much easier.

» Ask for help when grilling the meat or cooking on the stove.

## Kid Notes

» The potatoes may require a sharp knife for cutting into strips—please ask for assistance.

» Line pan with foil or parchment.

» Use a pastry brush and paint the chips with Paint Magic.

» Get help putting the pan in the oven and taking it out.

# Katie's Homemade Potato Chips

*4 medium potatoes*
*Paint Magic (page 128)*

**Yield: 6–8 servings**

- Preheat oven to 350°.

- Wash potatoes and cut in slices or long strips, skin on.

- Hint—Place potato strips in a bowl of ice water with ¼ cup white vinegar and soak for 10 minutes. Drain in colander. This will make them extra crisp!

- Place in single layer on a baking pan covered with aluminum foil or parchment. (We prefer parchment because aluminum foil tends to stick.)

- Brush with Paint Magic until well coated. (See recipe on page 128.)

- Bake for 20 minutes.

- Turn and brush again with Paint Magic.

- Bake for 45–50 minutes, until brown.

# Paint Magic

*½ cup olive oil*
*¼ cup fresh lemon juice*
*¼ cup Worcestershire sauce*
*Up to 5 garlic cloves*
*½ teaspoon black pepper*

## Yield: 1 cup

- Mix all the ingredients in a blender until smooth.

- Pour into a container with a top.

- Store in the refrigerator for up to 1 week.

- When ready to use brush it on vegetable or meat before and during cooking.

- May also be used as a dip, a marinade, or a sauce for meats and vegetables.

## Kid Notes

» Use your liquid measuring cup and measure all ingredients.

» Place all of the ingredients in the blender. Make sure the blender top is on tightly! Turn the blender on and "whirl" until smooth.

# Slow Cooked BBQ Baked Beans

*¼ pound bacon strips, cut into thirds*
*1 medium onion, finely chopped*
*3 14.5-ounce cans pork and beans*
*½ cup ketchup*
*1 cup light brown sugar, lightly packed*
*2 tablespoons prepared mustard*
*2 tablespoons Worcestershire sauce*
*3 shakes Tabasco sauce*

## Yield: 6–8 servings

- Cook bacon in a 4-quart pot until crisp. Drain all but 2 tablespoons of grease.

- Add onion and sauté until clear.

- Add beans and stir.

- Add remaining ingredients.

- Stir well and simmer uncovered until cooked down to desired consistency (about 2 hours).

## Kid Notes

» Have some help cooking the bacon and chopping the onion.

» Measure the ingredients and dump them in the pot.

» Stir well—read a book for 2 hours or begin making the hamburgers, French fries, and brownies for your backyard burger bash!

# Backyard Brown Sugar Brownies

### Brownie Mixture:
*2 ounces unsweetened chocolate*
*1 cup all-purpose flour, sifted*
*¼ teaspoon salt*
*¾ teaspoon cinnamon*
*½ teaspoon baking soda*
*⅔ cup butter*
*1¼ cups light brown sugar, packed*
*1 large egg*
*1 teaspoon vanilla*
*⅓ cup sour cream*
*1 cup pecans (optional)*

### Buttery Cinnamon Frosting:
*3 tablespoons butter, softened*
*1½ cups powdered sugar, sifted*
*¼ teaspoon cinnamon*
*Pinch of salt*
*1 tablespoon milk*
*½ teaspoon vanilla*

Yield: 9–12 brownies

- Preheat oven to 350°.

- Grease and flour an 8- or 9-inch square brownie pan.

- Melt unsweetened chocolate in a double boiler. Cool.

- Combine flour, salt, cinnamon, and baking soda. Sift and set aside.

- In a large bowl, cream butter with an electric mixer.

- Add sugar in thirds and continue to cream until fluffy.

- Add egg and beat until smooth. Stir in vanilla, sour cream, and melted chocolate.

- Fold in flour mixture. Stir in nuts, if desired.

- Bake in the center of oven 25–30 minutes or until top is dry and wooden toothpick inserted 1 inch from center comes out barely moist. Depending on the oven, it may take longer than 30 minutes to cook completely.

- Cool completely on a rack.

### For Buttery Cinnamon Frosting:

- Sift powdered sugar, cinnamon, and salt.

- With an electric mixer, cream butter. Add sifted ingredients. Mix well.

- Add milk and vanilla. Beat until fluffy.

- Spread on brownies. Cut into 2–3-inch squares.

## Kid Notes

» Chocolate needs to be slowly and gently heated. That is what a double boiler does; it won't scorch the chocolate (see Kid Notes on page 107).

» For ingredients like flour, sugar, salt, cinnamon, and baking soda use measuring cups and spoons in the exact measurement—for a half cup use 1/2-cup measuring cup. For a full cup use 1-cup measuring cup.

» Sifting the dry ingredients makes the measurement more consistent. Some flour is packed loosely and some is packed tightly. Sifting gives us the right amount.

» You can use the hand mixer or the standing mixer.

» When measuring the brown sugar, press down tightly in the measuring cup.

» Crack the egg in a separate bowl to make sure that there is no shell in the cracked eggs. Then add to the butter mixture. (See Kids Note on page 63.)

» When folding in the sifted flour mixture, do so by hand using a large rubber spatula. Scoop batter from the bottom of the bowl and then up the side of the bowl and up to the top. Repeat and turn bowl until the batter looks blended.

» Ask for help when placing the pan in and removing it from the oven.

» Make sure the brownies are completely cool before frosting.

# The Perfect Peach Blueberry Cobbler

*4–5 large peaches, peeled and sliced*
*3 tablespoons unsalted butter*
*1 tablespoon lemon juice*
*⅓ cup sugar*
*1 cup fresh blueberries*

## Topping:

*5 tablespoons unsalted butter*
*1 cup all-purpose flour*
*⅔ cup sugar*
*½ teaspoon salt*
*1½ teaspoons baking powder*
*1 cup heavy cream*
*1 egg yolk*
*Vanilla ice cream*

Yield: 6–8 servings

- Cut peaches into bite-sized pieces.

- Heat butter in a large skillet.

- Add the peaches, lemon juice, and sugar.

- Cook over medium heat until softened, 2–3 minutes.

- Gently toss in the blueberries.

## Kid Notes

» The peaches are easy to peel and slice with a plastic or table knife. It is best to do so on a cutting board.

» Ask for help cooking the peaches on the stove.

» Use a whisk to combine the dry ingredients.

» For instructions on separating eggs, see the Kid Notes on page 61.

» Ask for help when placing the cobbler in and removing it from the oven.

### For topping:

- Preheat oven to 350°. Place butter in a 9-inch square pan and put in oven to melt.

- Combine the flour, sugar, salt, and baking powder in a mixing bowl.

- Add the cream and egg yolk and mix well.

- Remove the baking pan from the oven and stir the butter into the batter, leaving just enough to coat the pan.

- Spoon the peaches and blueberries into the baking pan and pour the batter on top.

- Place in oven.

- Check after 25 minutes. If the top is brown, cover loosely with foil.

- Bake until a knife or toothpick inserted near the middle comes out clean. This usually takes 30–35 minutes.

- Cool.

- Serve warm with vanilla ice cream.

Note: May use frozen peaches and blueberries if fresh are not in season.

# pool party

Make a splash with this perfect-for-poolside or backyard party. Almost everything can be done ahead of time, and that's a good thing, because the pull of the pool commands the attention of even the best young kitchen helper. So much can be done the day or the morning before. The corn can be shucked, buttered, and wrapped. Re Re's Sand Cookies, one of Leslie's mom's tried and true summer recipes, can be made ahead. Prepare the potato salad without adding the mayonnaise, cover and refrigerate. Stir in the mayo before heading out to the pool. Annie's Sassy Salsa is just as colorful and sassy as its namesake, Leslie's daughter Annie. The chicken nuggets and corn dog skewers can be prepared up to the point of baking. Go for a dive; then dine.

Annie's Sassy Salsa
Baked Chicken Nuggets on a Stick
Oven Baked Corn Dog Skewers
On or Off the Grill Buttered Corn
Poolside Potato Salad
Summer Fruit Skewers with Caramel or Orange Fruit Dip
Re Re's Sand Cookies
Christina's Scrumptious Bread Pudding
with Fresh Berries

# Annie's Sassy Salsa

2 15-ounce cans black beans, drained and rinsed
1 16-ounce can white corn, drained
½ cup cilantro, finely chopped
¼ cup green onions, finely chopped
⅓ cup fresh lime juice
3 tablespoons olive oil
1 tablespoon cumin
½–1 teaspoon salt, to taste
Ground black pepper, to taste
1 4-ounce can chopped green chilies
4 dashes hot sauce (if desired)

**Yield: 6 cups**

- Combine above ingredients in order given and mix well.

- Refrigerate until ready to serve.

- Serve with tortilla chips or Frito Scoops.

## Kid Notes

» Drain and rinse the black beans in a colander in the sink.

» Use a lemon juicer for juicing the lime—it works for both.

» Dump and mix ingredients together and proudly serve this dip with your favorite chip. (We love Scoops.)

# Baked Chicken Nuggets on a Stick

*6 chicken breasts, boned and skinned*
*½ cup plain bread crumbs*
*¼ cup Parmesan cheese, grated*
*1 teaspoon garlic salt*
*½ cup butter, melted*
*wooden skewers*

## Yield: 6–8 servings

- Preheat oven to 400°.

- Soak wooden skewers in water for at least 20 minutes before using.

- Line a baking sheet with foil.

- Cut chicken into bite-sized chunks.

- Mix bread crumbs with Parmesan cheese and garlic salt.

- Dip chicken chunks into melted butter.

- Roll in crumb mixture.

- Stick 3 chicken chunks on a skewer. Lay on foil-lined baking sheet.

- Bake for 10–12 minutes.

## Kid Notes

» Be sure to wash your hands well before and after handling the raw chicken.

» Roll the chicken pieces in butter and crumbs.

» When skewering chicken, be careful not to stick yourself with the point.

» Line the pan with foil.

» Ask for help when placing the chicken in and removing it from the oven.

# Oven Baked Corn Dog Skewers

*3 tablespoons yellow cornmeal*
*1 11.5-ounce can refrigerated cornbread twists or*
  *breadsticks*
*1 tablespoon prepared mustard*
*8 hotdogs*
*wooden skewers*

**Yield: 8 servings**

- Preheat oven to 400°.

- Soak wooden skewers in water for at least 20 minutes before using.

- Sprinkle cornmeal on sheet of waxed paper.

- Separate dough into 8 long strips.

- Unroll dough on cornmeal; press into cornmeal.

- Spread dough with mustard.

- To make each corn dog, coil 1 dough strip around each hotdog.

- For extra crunchiness, roll again in cornmeal.

- Insert wooden skewer lengthwise through hotdog, securing dough on each end.

- Place corn dogs on a baking sheet lined with parchment paper.

- Bake for 12–15 minutes until golden brown.

## Kid Notes

» Unroll corn bread twist and press onto cornmeal. Then spread the dough with mustard and wrap.

» Watch out for the sharp point on the skewer when putting on hotdog.

» Ask for help when placing the pan in and removing it from the oven.

# On or Off the Grill Buttered Corn

*8 ears corn*
*½ cup butter*
*1 teaspoon Creole seasoning*
*8 12- by 8-inch squares of aluminum foil*

**Yield: 8 servings**

- Preheat oven to 350°.

- Remove the husks and silk from each ear of corn. Rinse corn and pat dry.

- Cut the butter into 8 equal pieces.

- Set one ear of corn on top of each piece of piece of foil. Place 1 pat of butter on corn and sprinkle with some of the Creole seasoning.

- Roll up the foil over the corn. Tuck in the sides. Place the corn on a baking sheet. Bake until tender, about 1 hour.

- Remove the baking sheet from the oven and let cool for 5 minutes before taking the corn out of the hot foil.

- Be careful unwrapping the foil from the hot corn— both the steam and the corn are hot!

- You may also cook on a medium-fire grill for about 45 minutes or until tender.

## Kid Notes

» Have a blast shucking the corn! For easier clean up, do it outside over a garbage bag.

» You can help decide if you want this yummy corn cooked inside or on the grill.

# Poolside Potato Salad

*2 pounds red new potatoes, cubed*
*2 tablespoons white vinegar*
*1 cup celery, finely chopped*
*½ cup onion, grated*
*¼ cup fresh parsley*
*4 hard-boiled eggs, chopped*
*1 teaspoon salt*
*¼ teaspoon pepper*
*½ teaspoon Creole seasoning*
*1½ cups mayonnaise*
*8 bacon slices, cooked, crisp and crumbled (optional)*

## Yield: 6 servings

- Cook potatoes in lightly salted water until tender (about 20 minutes).

- Drain in colander and rinse with cold water.

- When slightly cool, add celery, onion, parsley, and chopped eggs. Mix mayonnaise and vinegar together. Fold mayonnaise mixture into potato mixture. Season with salt, pepper, and Creole seasoning.

- Add bacon crumbles, if desired.

- Refrigerate until completely chilled.

## Kid Notes

» Ask an adult to help you drain the hot cooked potatoes in the colander.

» Basic recipe for hard-boiled eggs: Place eggs in a single layer in a pot and cover with warm water. Bring to a boil over high heat and immediately lower heat to lowest setting. Begin timing now. In 14 minutes remove from the stove and place in the sink. Run cold water into pot until the entire pot feels cool. Hard-boiled eggs will keep in their shells in the refrigerator for up to two weeks.

» Grate onion using downward strokes on the grater. Be careful at the end not to scrape your fingers on the grater—ouch!

» Chop celery, parsley, and eggs with a plastic knife or a table knife.

# Summer Fruit Skewers

## Kid Notes

» You don't need to spend lots of time peeling and chopping to make these colorful fruit kebabs. Instead of purchasing whole fruits, you can buy a container of sliced or cubed fruit from the grocery store.

*Bite-sized pieces of different fruits*
   *strawberries*
   *apple wedges*
   *grapes*
   *melon*
   *pineapple*
   *oranges*
   *kiwi chunks*
*Straws*

- To make each kebab, pinch the end of a straw and push it through a piece of fruit.

- Slide the fruit to the other end of the straw. You'll need 6–8 pieces per skewer.

- Add more fruit to fill the skewer with a range of colors.

- Individually cover each kebab with plastic.

- Wrap and refrigerate until it's time eat.

# Caramel Fruit Dip

*¼ cup sugar*
*¾ cup light brown sugar, packed*
*1 teaspoon vanilla extract*
*8 ounces cream cheese, softened*
*fresh fruit for dipping*

- Put sugars, vanilla, and cream cheese in blender or food processor and blend until smooth.

- Serve with a colorful assortment of seasonal fruit, such as apple slices, pear slices, and strawberries.

# Orange Cream Fruit Dip

*8 ounces cream cheese, softened*
*7 ounces marshmallow crème*
*2 tablespoons fresh orange juice*
*fresh fruit for dipping*

- *In a food processor or blender, mix all ingredients. Chill until ready to serve.*

## Kid Notes

» The fruit dips on this page make fresh fruit a real dessert!

» Place ingredients in food processor and pulse until blended—super easy and super good! (Remember to ask an adult for help.)

## Kid Notes

» You can use a hand mixer or a standing mixer for mixing the ingredients.

» Crack the egg in a small bowl first, if no shells then add to butter and sugar mixture. (See Kid Notes on page 63.)

» Measure the dry ingredients into a bowl and stir with a whisk.

» You can flatten all of the cookies out by yourself.

» Ask for help when placing the pan in and removing it from the oven.

# Re Re's Sand Cookies

1 cup sugar
½ cup butter
½ cup shortening
1 egg
2½ cups flour
¾ teaspoon salt
½ teaspoon baking soda
½ teaspoon baking powder
1 teaspoon vanilla extract
½ teaspoon almond extract
2 tablespoons milk
Sugar

**Yield: 24–30 cookies**

▪ Preheat oven to 350°.

▪ Line baking sheet with parchment paper.

▪ Beat butter and shortening together.

▪ Add 1 cup sugar gradually and make fluffy.

▪ Keep beating and add egg. Combine flour, salt, baking soda, and baking powder, stirring with a whisk. Slowly add dry ingredients to butter and egg mixture.

▪ Stir in extracts and milk and blend.

▪ Drop by tablespoons on a baking sheet.

▪ Dip  glass with a 2-3 inch bottom into a bowl of water, then a bowl of sugar and press each cookie, one by one, flat onto the baking sheet.

▪ Bake for 12 minutes.

# Christina's Scrumptious Bread Pudding with Fresh Berries

## Bread Pudding:

1 circular loaf of Hawaiian bread (1-pound loaf in tin)
2 cups heavy cream
1 cup milk
½ teaspoon vanilla extract
2 ounces white chocolate
7 egg yolks
½ cup sugar
1 teaspoon vanilla extract
2 pinches salt
Melted butter to coat pan

## White Chocolate Ganache:

10 ounces white chocolate
¾ cup heavy cream
1 teaspoon vanilla extract or brandy

## Berry Sauce:

1 pound frozen raspberries or mixed berries, defrosted and strained with excess juice reserved
Juice of half a lemon
2 tablespoons heavy cream
¼ cup sugar
Fresh berries (blueberries, raspberries, blackberries, and strawberries)

Yield: 8–10 servings

## Bread Pudding:

- Preheat oven to 350°.

- Tear Hawaiian bread into large chunks and place in a bowl.

- In a double boiler, melt white chocolate. Add the cream, milk, and ½ teaspoon vanilla extract. Whisk until combined. Continue to whisk occasionally. Cook until tiny bubbles form on the surface of the cream mixture. Do not let this mixture come to a boil. Remove from heat and cool.

- In a large mixing bowl, whisk egg yolks vigorously. Add sugar and continue to whisk till mixture has lightened in color. Stir in 1 teaspoon vanilla extract and salt.

- While whisking, slowly add cream mixture to the egg mixture.

- Pour over the bread and let sit for 5 minutes. Toss with hands to ensure that all bread has been coated.

- Coat a 9- by 13-inch pan with melted butter and pour mixture into pan.

- Place a sheet of parchment paper over pan and bake for 30 minutes. Remove parchment paper and bake for another 10 minutes. While bread pudding is baking, prepare the sauces.

### White Chocolate Ganache:

- Chop white chocolate and place in a medium-sized mixing bowl.

- In a saucepan, heat cream and vanilla extract over medium heat until small bubbles begin to form. Do not bring this mixture to a boil.

- Remove cream mixture from heat and immediately pour over white chocolate. Let stand for 5 minutes so that chocolate melts.

- After five minutes, stir the white chocolate ganache until all the chocolate is melted.

- If you are making this sauce in advance and keeping it in the refrigerator, make sure to microwave the sauce for about 30 seconds before pouring over the bread pudding.

### Berry Sauce:

- Drain defrosted berries and reserve juice.

- Place berries in a blender or cuisinart and blend with lemon juice, cream, and sugar.

- Strain well, making sure no seeds are left. If sauce looks too thick, simply add some of the reserved berry juice to thin out the sauce.

- The sauce should taste somewhat tart in order to complement the sweetness of the white chocolate ganache.

- Serve with warmed white chocolate ganache and berry sauce. Garnish with fresh berries. A real treat!

## Kid Notes

» For making your own double boiler, see Kid Notes on page 107.

» This recipe seems long, but it is not hard. It is really a lot of fun—and worth it!

» To learn how to separate an egg, see Kid Notes on page 61. You can save the seven egg whites for another recipe. Place in a covered container in the refrigerator for up to 4 days.

» It works really well to put each sauce into a squirt bottle and drizzle over the bread pudding. You can even make designs on the serving plate!

» If you have extra sauce, you can make an entirely new dessert by drizzling either or both sauces over vanilla ice cream.

» Garnish with your choice of fresh berries.

# pizza parlor!

Forget about the pizza delivery man. Deliver your own family fun with "design your own" pizzas using ingredients and leftovers from your own refrigerator. Old and young family members alike take pride in creating a custom pizza. In our homes, pizza is a favorite meal any time of the day—including breakfast. "Design Your Own" pizzas have long been a favorite activity for Helen and her son Martin. Even as a small child, he and his neighborhood friends were fascinated with watching the yeast bubble and the dough rise. They loved "patting" the dough into round discs and, most of all, adding the toppings all by themselves. Helen likes to turn the pizza making into even more of a party by putting ingredients and toppings in small bowls on the kitchen counter, so each child and grown-up can easily create their own personal pizza.

Perfect Pizza Crust

Best BBQ Chicken Pizza!

Design Your Own!

Farm Fresh Pizza

It Only Takes A Minute Pizza

Everyone Loves Cookie Pizza!

All American Green Apple Pizza

# Perfect Pizza Crust

1 package active dry yeast
1¼ cups lukewarm water
1 tablespoon honey
3 tablespoons extra-virgin olive oil
1 teaspoon salt
3½ cups all-purpose flour
½ cup bread flour, for kneading

**Yield: Crust for an 8-serving pizza**

- In a large bowl, combine the yeast, warm water, and honey. Set aside until foamy, about 10 minutes.

- Mix together all-purpose flour and salt. Add oil to mixture.

- Slowly add yeast mixture to flour and salt mixture, using a wooden spoon. Stir to combine, making sure to incorporate all ingredients.

- Transfer the dough to a surface sprinkled with bread flour.

- Knead dough and add remaining bread flour until it is smooth and elastic, 5–7 minutes.

- Cover the dough with a clean dishtowel and set aside to rise in a warm, draft-free place until doubled in size—about 1½ hours.

- Punch down the dough. On a lightly floured surface, using a floured rolling pin, roll dough into a circle the size of your pizza pan. Place in a pizza pan sprayed with nonstick cooking spray. Add the toppings of your choice and bake in a 400° oven for directed time.

## Kid Notes

» The water that you add to the yeast and honey should be warm (like a baby's bath), not hot.

» Once you see bubbles and foam in the yeast mixture it is ready to add to the flour. If there are no bubbles, throw it out and start with a new package of yeast. (Sometimes it just flops and that is okay.)

» Knead dough by pressing with the heel of your hand and folding over and over on a lightly floured surface until smooth and elastic. It helps to grease your hands to prevent sticking. This step requires muscles!

» Allow dough to rest while you have play time!

» Give the dough a few good punches then use a lightly floured rolling pin and roll dough out to fit your pizza pan.

» Add toppings just the way you like on your pizza!

## Kid Notes

» Wash your hands before and after handling the chicken.

» Ask for help when sautéing the chicken on the stove top.

» Arrange the ingredients on the pizza crust.

» Also, have an adult help you when placing the pizza in the oven and taking out of the oven.

# Best BBQ Chicken Pizza!

2 pounds chicken
½ cup barbecue sauce
1½ teaspoons olive oil
1 cup mozzarella cheese, shredded
½ cup smoked Gouda cheese, grated
½ cup red onion, sliced
2 teaspoons fresh cilantro, finely chopped
Pizza crust

## Yield: 8 servings

- Cut the chicken into bite-sized cubes and marinate it in ¼ cup of the barbecue sauce in the refrigerator for at least 2 hours.

- When the chicken has marinated, preheat the oven to 400°. Heat a small frying pan on your stove with 1½ teaspoons of olive oil in it. Sauté the chicken in the pan for 4–5 minutes until tender.

- Pat out your pizza crust onto a 9- by 13-inch baking sheet or pizza pan, and spread the remaining ¼ cup of the barbecue sauce evenly over the pizza crust.

- Sprinkle ½ cup of the mozzarella and all of the Gouda cheese over the sauce.

- Place the chicken and red onion on top.

- Sprinkle the remaining ½ cup mozzarella around the center of the pizza.

- The cilantro goes on top of the mozzarella.

- Bake the pizza for 10–12 minutes or until the crust is light brown.

- When the pizza is done, remove it from the oven and make 4 even cuts across the pie. This will give you 8 slices.

# Farm Fresh Pizza

## Crust:
*2 cups all-purpose flour*
*1½ teaspoons baking powder*
*1 teaspoon sugar*
*½ teaspoon salt*
*¼ cup butter, cut into small pieces*
*¾ cup cheddar cheese, grated*
*¾ cup milk*

## Topping:
*1 tablespoon butter*
*8 large eggs, lightly beaten*
*Salt and pepper to taste*
*1 16-ounce tube sausage, browned, drained, and crumbled, or 1 pound bacon,*
  *cooked and crumbled*
*1½ cup cheddar cheese, grated*

Yield: 6–8 servings

- Sift the flour, baking powder, sugar, and salt into a large mixing bowl.

- Using a pastry blender or your fingers, cut or rub the butter into the dry ingredients until it is broken into very small pieces.

- Add ¾ cup of cheese and toss lightly. Make a well in the dry ingredients, then add the milk. Stir gently just until the dough is mixed; then let it sit for several minutes.

- Preheat oven to 400°.

- Butter a 12-inch round pizza pan.

- Dust the dough and your hands with flour, then place the dough in the middle of the pizza pan and press it into a circle, touching the edge of pan. Pinch the edge into a slightly raised rim.

- Bake for 12–15 minutes until the top of the crust is a light golden brown.

- Meanwhile, prepare your topping ingredients. Brown the sausage or bacon in a skillet over medium heat. Remove with slotted spoon and drain on a paper towel.

- Using a large skillet, melt the butter over medium-low heat.

- Add the beaten eggs and scramble them lightly, adding salt and pepper to taste. Immediately remove eggs from the heat.

- Spoon the eggs over the baked crust, spreading them with a fork. Top with the sausage or bacon and cheese. Return the pan to the oven and bake 5 minutes longer until the cheese has melted. Slice and serve right away.

## Kid Notes

» The crust on this pizza is like a biscuit—handle gently instead of kneading.

» Ask for help when placing the biscuit dough in and removing it from the oven.

» When cracking eggs use two bowls. Crack the egg on the side of one bowl; use both hands to pull the egg apart. Allow the egg white and yolk to fall in the first bowl. If there is no shell, transfer the egg to the second bowl. Continue until all of the eggs are cracked.

» You are probably the greatest egg scrambler in the world, but do have an adult around when cooking on the stove top.

# Design Your Own!

*1 refrigerated canned pizza crust*
*Pizza sauce, as needed*
*Choice of toppings:*
  *pepperoni*
  *Canadian bacon*
  *broccoli*
  *bacon (cooked and crumbled)*
  *hamburger meat (browned)*
  *mushrooms*
  *fresh basil*
  *roasted red peppers*
  *Parmesan cheese*
  *mozzarella cheese*
  *cheddar cheese*
  *black olives*

## Yield: 8 servings

- Preheat oven to 400°.

- Open can of pizza crust and press into pizza pan. Bake for 5 minutes. Remove from oven.

- Spread pizza sauce on crust.

- Design with your favorite topping. Bake for 10–12 minutes until brown. Enjoy!

## Kid Notes

» When pressing the canned dough into the pizza pan, it is best to use your fingertips to push and pull.

» Have a blast arranging your toppings!

# It Only Takes a Minute Pizza

*1 16.3-ounce can refrigerated big biscuits*
*Choice of toppings:*
   *pepperoni*
   *Canadian bacon*
   *mushrooms*
   *black olives*
*1 cup of pizza sauce, store bought*
*1½ cups mozzarella cheese, grated*

**Yield: 8 servings**

- Preheat oven to 400°.

- Open the can of biscuits and have the children flatten the biscuits into discs by patting the biscuit dough between their hands.

- Place flattened disc on a baking sheet that has been sprayed with cooking spray or lined with parchment paper.

- Allow the children to "decorate" their individual little pizzas with their favorite toppings.

- Bake for 10–12 minutes, or until brown.

- Enjoy!

## Kid Notes

» This is your special, do it all by myself, I am so hungry and I can't wait much longer pizza!

» Follow the directions and make it just right for you!

» Do ask an adult to help you put the pizza in and take out of the oven.

# Everyone Loves Cookie Pizza!

## Pizza Crust:
2 eggs
1 cup light brown sugar, packed
½ cup granulated sugar
1 cup butter, softened
2 teaspoon vanilla
2½ cups flour
1 teaspoon baking soda

## Chocolate Pizza Sauce:
3 cups confectioners' sugar, sifted
3 tablespoons cocoa powder, sifted
4 tablespoons milk
4 tablespoons butter, softened
1 teaspoon vanilla extract
Pinch salt

## Toppings:
Choose from these topping ideas: multicolored sprinkles, colored sugar, mini chocolate chips, gummy worms, silver balls, mini-marshmallows, M&M's

Yield: 16 servings

- Preheat the oven to 350°. Spray the pizza pan with nonstick cooking spray.

- Mix the egg, brown sugar, granulated sugar, butter, and vanilla together. Stir with a wooden spoon until mixed.

- Add the flour and baking soda to sugar mixture.

- Spread or pat the dough into the greased pizza pan, using the back of a spoon or a piece of waxed paper pressed with your hand.

- Bake for about 15-20 minutes or until the crust is golden brown. Allow to cool.

- While the crust is cooling, make the chocolate pizza sauce. In a large mixing bowl, cream the butter, confectioners' sugar, and cocoa. Add the milk, vanilla extract, and salt and beat until smooth. Spread on cooled pizza crust. This sauce will keep in a covered container in the refrigerator for about one week.

- Right away, sprinkle with the candies. Add your choice of other candies if you like.

Tip: May use 1 tube of refrigerated sugar cookie dough. Pat into pizza pan and bake for 10–12 minutes.

## Kid Notes

» This is like a big cookie cake—decorate with your favorite toppings and have fun!

» If you are pressed for time, ready-made frosting will do fine.

# All American Green Apple Pizza

## Crust and Topping
2 cups all-purpose flour
2 cups quick-cooking rolled oats
1½ cups light brown sugar, packed
1 teaspoon baking soda
1¼ cups margarine or butter, melted

## Filling
1½ cups caramel ice cream topping
½ cup all-purpose flour
2 cups Granny Smith apples, peeled
    and coarsely chopped

Yield: 8 servings

- Heat oven to 350°.

- Grease  15- by 10- by 1-inch baking pan or round pizza pan.

- In large bowl, combine all crust and topping ingredients; mix until crumbly.

- Press half of mixture (about 2½ cups) in bottom of greased pan to form base.

- Reserve remaining mixture for topping. Bake at 350° for 8 minutes.

- Meanwhile, in small saucepan, combine caramel topping and ½ cup flour; blend well.

- Bring to a boil over medium heat, stirring constantly. Boil 3–5 minutes, or until mixture thickens slightly, stirring constantly.

- Remove pan from oven. Sprinkle apples over warm base. Pour caramel mixture evenly over top. Sprinkle with reserved topping mixture.

- Return to oven; bake an additional 25–30 minutes or until golden brown. Cool at room temperature for 30 minutes.

- Refrigerate 30 minutes or until set.

- Cut into slices.

## Kid Notes

» You will need assistance if using a sharp knife to cut the apples.

» A fork works great when combining the crust and topping ingredients.

» Ask an adult to help you put the pizza in and take out of the oven, as well as boil the caramel.

» This is delicious served with vanilla ice cream.

# soup by the spoonfuls

Stirring a pot of soup stirs up memories for most of us. There is nothing like a loving spoonful of soup to make us feel warm, secure, and nourished. When we teach the children in our classes to make soup, we know that we are helping them create memories that will last a lifetime. Making soup is a rewarding group experience—whether in a cooking class or in the family kitchen. Roll Over and Play Sick Soup is a vegetable soup handed down from Leslie's mother-in-law Marsh and served when anyone in the family is sick. Phillip, Leslie's husband, loves to eat Cheese Soup out of the Edible Bread Bowl, a tasty and whimsical container for any favorite soup. Hearty Chili was passed along by Helen's younger brother, Todd, who made this soup for his children's entire elementary school—and there wasn't a drop left in the pot.

Phillip's Cheese Soup

Flavorful Tortilla Soup

Cozy Cream of Tomato Soup

Roll Over and Play Sick Soup

Simple Shrimp Chowder

Hearty Chili

Edible Bread Bowl

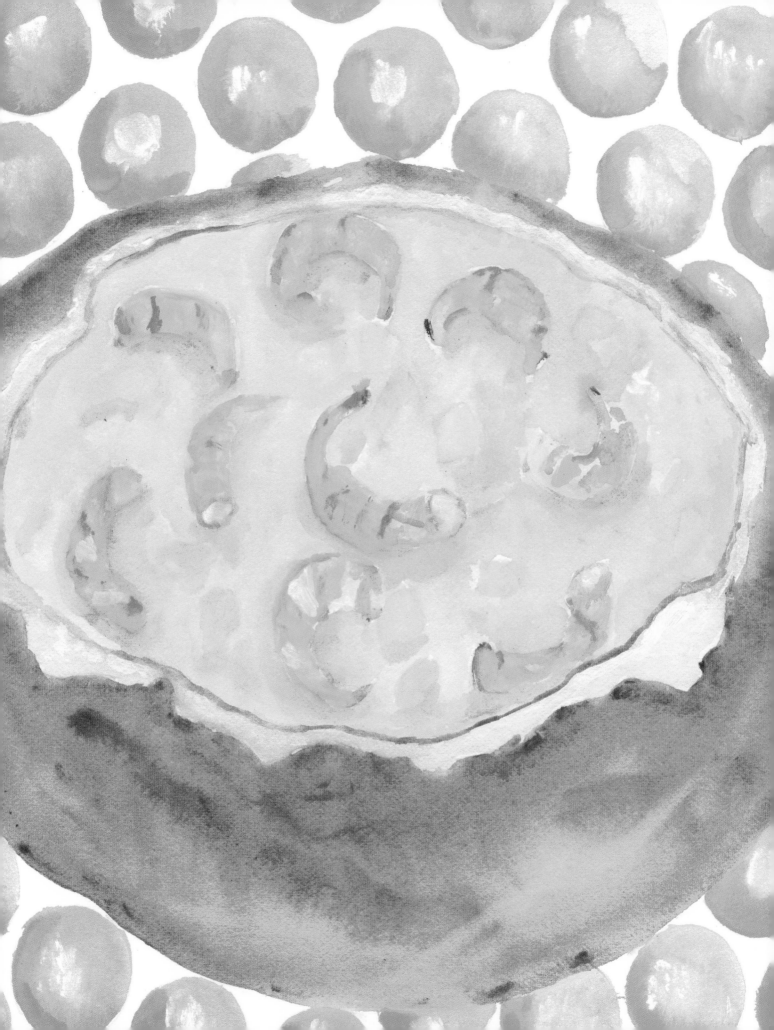

# Phillip's Cheese Soup

*4 tablespoons butter, melted*
*½ cup carrots, finely chopped*
*½ cup green pepper, finely chopped*
*½ cup onion, finely chopped*
*½ cup celery, finely chopped*
*½ cup flour*
*3 cans chicken broth*
*12 ounces medium cheddar cheese, grated (3 cups)*
*4 cups milk*
*Salt and white pepper, to taste*

## Yield: 8 servings

- In soup pot, melt butter. Add vegetables and simmer until tender but not browned. Whisk in the flour and cook, stirring, 1 minute.

- Add broth and cook, stirring, until thickened. Turn heat to low.

- Add cheese and cook, stirring, until melted.

- Stir in milk and bring to a simmer. Season to taste.

## Kid Notes

» Chop veggies very fine so that the soup will be velvety—you can use a mini-chopper.

» Open the cans of chicken broth and measure the flour.

» Using a whisk will help create a smooth soup.

» Use your best grating techniques (see Kid Notes page 41).

» Cheese does scorch— make sure to stir often and keep the heat low when adding the cheese.

# Flavorful Tortilla Soup

6 cups water
6 chicken breasts
2 onions, chopped
2 bay leaves
1 teaspoon salt
1 teaspoon pepper
4 cloves garlic, chopped
3 ribs celery, chopped
1 green pepper, chopped
1 jalapeno, seeded and chopped
2 tablespoons olive oil
1 can tomato soup

1 can Rotel tomatoes
1 teaspoon cumin
2 teaspoons chili powder
½ teaspoon salt
½ teaspoon pepper
1 tablespoon Worcestershire sauce
3 corn tortillas, cut into thin strips

**For garnishing:**
Cheddar cheese, grated
Monterey Jack cheese, grated
Sour cream

Yield: 8–10 servings

- In a large stock pot, cook chicken breast in water with one onion, bay leaves, salt, and pepper. Bring to a boil, reduce heat and simmer for 30 minutes.

- Turn off heat and allow breasts to begin to cool in broth for 30 minutes. Remove chicken from broth and cut into bite-sized pieces. Save broth. This may be done a day ahead of time.

- Sauté the garlic, onion, celery, bell pepper, and jalapeno in olive oil for 2 minutes. Add 4 cups chicken broth, tomato soup, Rotel tomatoes, and seasonings.

- Simmer on medium heat for 30 minutes.

- Add chicken pieces and Worcestershire sauce, salt, and pepper and cook for 15 minutes. Add tortilla strips and cook for 5 minutes.

- Serve with grated cheddar or Monterey Jack cheese, and a dollop of sour cream.

## Kid Notes

» This is a flavorful soup with lots of ingredients to chop. Using a food processor makes this job a cinch—just pulse the veggies until chopped fine.

» While the soup is simmering, measure the dry seasonings (cumin, chili powder, salt, and pepper) into a small bowl. You can add at once with the chicken pieces.

» Cut the tortillas into thin strips.

» Grate the cheese (see Kid Notes page 41).

# Cozy Cream of Tomato Soup

*3 tablespoons olive oil*
*1 large onion, finely chopped*
*1 28-ounce can crushed tomatoes, undrained*
*2 cups tomato juice*
*½ teaspoon salt*
*¼ teaspoon pepper*
*1 cup heavy cream*

## Yield: 8 servings

- In soup pot, over medium heat, sauté onion in olive oil until tender, about 4–5 minutes.

- Add can of crushed tomatoes and tomato juice.

- Simmer for 25 minutes.

- Add cream, salt, and pepper.

- Gently heat through.

- Serve warm.

## Kid Notes

» It is easier to chop the onion fine when using a food processor.

» Open the can of tomatoes with a can opener.

» Measure the cream into a liquid measuring cup.

» When sautéing, be sure not to touch the hot pot or stove top with your free hand. If you need help, ask an adult.

# Roll Over and Play Sick Soup

*2 pounds round steak, cut into bite-sized pieces*
*1 tablespoon olive oil*
*2 medium onions, chopped*
*1½ cups celery, chopped*
*6 medium carrots, peeled and sliced*
*1 10-ounce package frozen sliced okra*
*1 10-ounce package frozen baby lima beans*
*1 10-ounce package frozen corn*
*3 14.5-ounce cans beef broth*
*2 cans Rotel tomatoes*
*2 bay leaves*
*1 teaspoon salt*
*1 teaspoon pepper*
*2 teaspoons spicy spaghetti seasoning (or Italian seasoning)*
*1 teaspoon Creole seasoning*
*1 tablespoon soy sauce*

**Yield: 12–15 servings**

- In a large Dutch oven, cook steak and onion in olive oil until the meat is brown, about 5–7 minutes.

- Add celery, carrots, okra, lima beans, corn, beef broth, and tomatoes. Mix well to distribute ingredients.

- Stir in bay leaves, salt, pepper, spaghetti seasoning, Creole seasoning, and soy sauce.

- Bring soup to a boil. Then turn to low and simmer, covered, for 2½–3 hours.

- If necessary, add water to the soup.

Note: This soup may be prepared several days ahead and gets better with time! It freezes well.

## Kid Notes

» The meat is tender and not too hard to cut—just wash your hands before and after handling.

» The onions and celery can be chopped in a food processor.

» Be sure to scrape down the length of the carrot when peeling.

» This soup is sure to make anyone feel better!

# Simple Shrimp Chowder

1 tablespoon butter
1 onion, chopped fine
2 10¾-ounce cans cream of potato soup, undiluted
3¼ cups milk
½ teaspoon liquid crab boil
¼ teaspoon ground red pepper
⅛ teaspoon salt
1½ pounds medium-sized fresh or frozen shrimp,
    thawed
1 cup Monterey Jack cheese, shredded

Yield: 6–8 servings

- Melt butter in a heavy soup pan. Sauté onion over medium heat for 5 minutes until translucent.

- Using a whisk, stir in soup, milk, crab boil, red pepper, and salt. Slowly bring to a boil, stirring often.

- Add the shrimp, reduce heat, and simmer for about 4–5 minutes until shrimp turn pink.

- Add cheese and stir until melted and blended.

- Serve.

Note: 1½ pounds peeled crawfish tails may be used instead of shrimp.

## Kid Notes

» You will impress everyone with this easy and delicious soup.

» Chopping the onion fine is made easy in a food processor.

» Open the soup cans.

» Measure the milk in a liquid measuring cup.

» For crawfish chowder, add crawfish instead of shrimp.

# Hearty Chili

1  28-ounce cans crushed tomatoes
1 can Rotel tomatoes
2 cups water
3 pounds coarsely ground lean beef
1 large onion, chopped
2 cloves garlic
2 bay leaves, broken
1 teaspoon oregano
2 teaspoons ground cumin
1 teaspoon salt
3 tablespoons chili powder
2 teaspoons black pepper
1 tablespoon Southwest seasoning
2 tablespoons fresh cilantro
1–3 tablespoons flour (if needed for thickening)

## Yield: 10–12 servings

- In a soup pot blend water and tomatoes and let simmer over medium heat.

- Drain and add to tomato mixture. Add garlic, bay leaves, oregano, cumin, salt, chili powder, and pepper. Bring to a boil and reduce heat. Let simmer for 2½–3 hours.

- Add water if the chili gets too thick during cooking. Add cilantro 30 minutes before chili is ready. If needed, mix in flour to thicken.

## Kid Notes

» Be careful chopping the onions and sautéing the ground beef.

» Add all of the ingredients and know that in just a couple of hours you and your family will sit down to a great bowl of chili.

» You can adjust the seasonings to make it hot or mild—as it is, it is just right.

# Edible Bread Bowl

*1 loaf frozen bread dough, thawed but still cold*
*1 egg, beaten*

### Yield: 4 bowls

- Cut loaf into fourths. Form into balls. Place on a sprayed baking pan at least 2 inches apart.
- Use a pastry brush to brush tops with beaten egg.
- Cover loaves with a piece of plastic sprayed with nonstick cooking spray. Let dough rise to double in size. Remove plastic wrap.
- Bake at 350° for 25 minutes.
- Allow to cool.
- Cut a hole in the top and hollow out insides.
- Fill with your favorite soup.
- Save hollowed bread for dipping in soup.
- Enjoy!

Note: Can be made a day before using.

## Kid Notes

» This is a fun way to serve soup—no washing the bowl, just eat it along with the soup that is in it.

» Use a pastry brush to brush the bread with the beaten egg.

» Use a serrated knife to cut the hole in the bread top. You will need an adult to help you.

» Leave enough thickness around the bottom and sides of the bowl so it will be strong enough to hold the soup.

# Kitchen Notes

# keep your eyes on pies

Pies are known to disappear from the family table before your very eyes. It doesn't matter if it's savory or sweet, everyone loves a pie! From start to finish, your little helper will be engaged and involved in the creation of one of these versatile and delicious pies. Tastiest Toffee Ice Cream Pie is a favorite of Helen and her son, Martin. They learned to make it when they lived in the sunny California community of Palos Verdes. William's Deep Dish Pizza Pie was created by Leslie to please her son, who wants pizza for every meal. The Sweetheart Fudge Pie with a delicious cream cheese crust is a prize-winning recipe from Leslie's mom, and Susie Shepherd's Pie is a can't-keep-on-the-shelf item at Leslie's aunt's gourmet-to-go shop in New Orleans.

Comfy Chicken Pot Pie
Favorite Sloppy Joe Pie
Susie Shepherd's Pie
William's Deep Dish Pizza Pie
Classic Chicken Spaghetti Pie

My Oh My Apple Pie
Tastiest Toffee Ice Cream Pie
Old Fashioned Pecan Pie
Delightful Cheese Pie
Sweetheart Fudge Pie

Cream Cheese Pie Crust
Graham Cracker Pie Crust
Chocolate Wafer Pie Crust
Homemade Pie Crust

# Comfy Chicken Pot Pie

*2 ready-made pie crusts, or make your own pie crusts
  (see page 181)*
*⅓ cup margarine or butter*
*⅓ cup onion, chopped*
*⅓ cup all-purpose flour*
*½ teaspoon salt*
*¼ teaspoon pepper*
*¼ teaspoon Creole seasoning*
*1 14-ounce can of chicken broth*
*⅓ cup milk*
*2½ cups cooked chicken, shredded*
*1¾ cups frozen mixed vegetables, thawed*

## Yield: 6 servings

- Heat oven to 425°.

- Melt butter in medium saucepan over medium heat. Add onion; cook and stir 2 minutes or until tender.

- Add flour, salt, Creole seasoning, and pepper; whisk until well blended. Gradually stir in broth and milk, cooking and stirring with a whisk until bubbly and thickened.

- Add chicken and mixed vegetables; mix well. Remove from heat.

- Spoon chicken and vegetable mixture into crust-lined pan. Top with second crust; seal edges and flute crimp. Cut slits in several places in top crusts.

- Bake at 425° for 30–40 minutes or until crust is golden brown. Cover edge of crust with strips of foil during last 15–20 minutes of baking if necessary to prevent excessive browning.

- Let stand 5 minutes before serving.

## Kid Notes

» Ask for help chopping the onion.

» Also get an adult to help you cook the white sauce on the stove. Be sure to use a whisk—it will make the sauce smooth.

» After boiling the chicken save the liquid and use as the chicken broth asked for in the recipe.

» Chop the cooked chicken with a plastic or table knife.

» When sealing the edges, press your thumb and index finger of the hand against the rim of the pan, then poke your other index finger through the space between your thumb and index finger; or use the lines of a fork to press all around the rim of the pan.

» Ask for help when placing the pie in and removing it from the oven.

## Kid Notes

» Chop the green onions with a plastic or table knife.

» Ask for help cooking beef and green onions on the stove top.

» Cut the biscuits in half with a plastic or table knife. Arrange on top of the Sloppy Joe mixture in the pan.

» Have an adult help you place the pie in the oven and take out of the oven.

# Favorite Sloppy Joe Pie

*1½ pounds lean ground beef*
*½ cup green onions, sliced*
*1 15.5-ounce can Sloppy Joe sauce*
*1 11-ounce can Mexican whole kernel corn, undrained*
*1 6-ounce can (5 biscuits) refrigerated buttermilk flaky biscuits*

## Yield: 6–8 servings

- Preheat oven to 375°.

- In a large skillet, cook ground beef and onions until beef is browned and thoroughly cooked, stirring frequently. Drain.

- Stir in sauce. Cook for 4–5 minutes, or until thoroughly heated, stirring occasionally. Spoon mixture into ungreased 9-inch glass pie plate.

- Separate biscuits; cut each in half. Arrange cut side down around outside edge of Sloppy Joe mixture with sides of biscuits touching.

- Bake at 375° for 15–20 minutes or until biscuits are brown.

# Susie Shepherd's Pie

## Mashed Potato Topping:

6 cups potatoes, peeled and cubed
2 teaspoons salt, plus salt to taste
4 tablespoons butter, cut into pieces
1 cup sour cream
¼ cup milk

## Filling:

2 pounds ground beef
½ cup flour
1 tablespoon Creole seasoning
1 tablespoon Italian seasoning
¼ teaspoon pepper
¾ cup onions, chopped
½ cup green onions, chopped
3 tablespoons garlic, chopped
1½ cups beef broth

## Cheese Topping

1½–2 cups cheddar cheese, grated
Fresh parsley, chopped, for garnish on top
Paprika, for sprinkling on top

Yield: 2 pies

## Kid Notes

» Peel potatoes in downward position, turning the potatoes.

» Ask for help when boiling potatoes and draining them.

» Onions are hard to chop—ask for help when using a sharp knife.

» Have an adult assist with cooking the onions and ground beef on the stove top, as well as with the rest of the stove top cooking.

» Have fun mixing the potatoes with the hand mixer.

» Ask an adult to help put the pie in the oven and take it out of the oven.

- Peel potatoes and cube. Place potatoes in a large pot with enough water to cover them by a couple of inches. Add 2 teaspoons of salt to the water. Bring the potatoes to a boil, uncovered, over high heat. Cook them for 10–12 minutes.

- Begin the filling while the potatoes cook.

- Preheat oven to 350°.

- Sauté ground beef, adding flour after meat starts to brown.

- Add seasoning, onions, peppers, and garlic.

- Continue to brown and wilt vegetables, stirring.

- Add the beef broth and continue to cook until you have a moist beef mixture that is thick and wet.

- Adjust seasoning.

- Spray a baking pan or pie dish with nonstick cooking spray.

- Place beef mixture on bottom.

- The potatoes are done if easily cut with a butter knife. Drain the potatoes in a colander.

- Place the drained potatoes in a large mixing bowl and add the butter pieces and the sour cream over the hot potatoes. Allow the butter to melt and the sour cream to warm so the ingredients will be easier to blend, then partially mash the potatoes with a hand masher or a large fork.

- Switch to an electric mixer set at medium speed and continue to mash, adding enough milk to make medium-soft mashed potatoes.

- Add salt to taste to the potatoes and spoon them evenly over the beef mixture.

- Top with cheese and garnishes.

- Bake for 15–20 minutes, until thoroughly warmed and cheese is melted.

# William's Deep Dish Pizza Pie

*1 pound lean ground beef*
*¾ cup onion, finely chopped*
*1 8-ounce jar pizza sauce*
*1 11-ounce can refrigerated crusty French loaf*
*1 cup mozzarella cheese, shredded*
*1 cup Parmesan cheese, shredded*
*1 3-ounce package sliced pepperoni*
*1 egg*
*1 tablespoon water*

Yield: 8 servings

- Preheat oven to 350°. Spray 9-inch glass pie plate with nonstick cooking spray. In medium skillet, cook ground beef and onion over medium-high heat for 5–7 minutes or until beef is thoroughly cooked. Drain. Stir in pizza sauce until well mixed.

- Carefully unroll dough. Place in sprayed pie pan so edges extend over sides of pan, leaving dough extended over sides. Spoon ground beef mixture into crust. On top, layer half of the mozzarella and Parmesan, the pepperoni slices, and then the remaining cheese.

- In small bowl, slightly beat egg and water with a fork. Fold extended edges of dough up and over filling; seal edges. Brush crust with egg mixture using a pastry brush.

- Bake for 40 minutes or until deep golden brown. Cool for 15 minutes. To serve, slice into wedges. Serve with additional pizza sauce, if desired.

## Kid Notes

» Ask for help cutting the onion and cooking it with the beef on the stove top.

» Open the can of dough, unroll it, and place in the pie pan, leaving the edges hanging off the sides.

» Spoon filling onto the dough and top with the pepperoni and cheeses.

» Fold the dough over the top of the filling and pinch it together to seal it closed.

» Crack the egg in a bowl and mix with a fork. (See Kids Notes on page 63.)

» "Paint" the beaten egg on the crust of the pizza using a pastry brush.

» Ask for help when placing the pizza in and removing it from the oven.

# Classic Chicken Spaghetti Pie

*2 pounds boneless, skinless chicken breast*
*2  14-ounce cans cream of mushroom soup*
*1 bell pepper, finely chopped*
*½ cup celery, finely chopped*
*2 cloves garlic, minced*
*2 onions, finely chopped*
*1 tablespoon butter*
*1  16-ounce package spaghetti*
*1 egg, beaten*
*⅓ cup almonds, slivered (optional)*
*⅓ cup cooking sherry*
*1 tablespoon Worcestershire sauce*
*Salt and pepper, to taste*
*1 cup Parmesan cheese, shredded*

**Yield: 2 pies**

- In a large stock pot, cover the chicken with water and bring to a boil. Reduce heat and simmer for 20 minutes. Remove chicken from stock. Cool and chop into bite-sized pieces.

- Preheat oven to 350°.

- Lightly grease two 9-inch glass pie plates.

- Sauté the bell peppers, onions, celery, and garlic in 1 tablespoon butter until soft, about 2 minutes. Add cream of mushroom soup and stir.

- Boil spaghetti in chicken stock until al dente and drain.

- Mix spaghetti, egg, sautéed vegetables, and chicken.

- Add the almonds, sherry, Worcestershire sauce, salt, and pepper. Mix well. Put in glass pie plates.

- Cover with Parmesan cheese.

- Bake for 30–40 minutes until bubbly.

## Kid Notes

» Chop the bell pepper, celery, garlic, and onion while the chicken is cooking. You may use a garlic press for the garlic.

» Make sure chicken is cool before chopping—save the broth for cooking the spaghetti.

» Have an adult assist you in sautéing the veggies on the stove top.

» Crack the egg in a bowl and stir with a fork. (See Kids Notes on page 63.)

» Stir all of the spaghetti ingredients together. Add Worcestershire, salt, and pepper.

» Cover the top with Parmesan cheese. (You can grate the cheese yourself or purchase it already grated.)

# My Oh My Apple Pie

*5 cups apples, sliced, peeled, cored, and divided*
*1½ cups of light brown sugar, lightly packed*
*⅓ cup water*
*1 cup all-purpose flour*
*¾ cup butter*
*1½ teaspoons cinnamon*

## Yield: 8 servings

- Preheat oven to 350°.

- Place apple slices in a 9-inch glass pie plate that has been sprayed with nonstick cooking spray.

- Sprinkle ½ cup of sugar on top of the apples.

- Pour water over the sugar and apples.

- Place remaining ingredients in food processor. Pulse until crumbly and sprinkle evenly over apples.

- Bake for 40–45 minutes.

## Kid Notes

» Peel and core apples, then slice.

» Spray the pie plate with nonstick cooking spray.

» Measure brown sugar in a dry measuring cup.

» Measure water in a liquid measuring cup—pour over apples.

» Put flour and remaining 1 cup brown sugar in the food processor and pulse until crumbly. Sprinkle over the apples, sugar, and water.

» Ask for help when placing the apple pie in and removing it from the oven.

# Tastiest Toffee Ice Cream Pie

### Toffee Ice Cream Pie:
*1 Chocolate Wafer Crust (see page 180), unbaked*
*6 ounces chocolate toffee candy bars (Heath bars)*
*1 pint Vanilla ice cream*

### Chocolate Silk Sauce:
*¼ cup butter, melted*
*1 cup milk chocolate chips*
*1¼ cups powdered sugar*
*1 5½-ounce can evaporated milk*
*1 teaspoon vanilla extract*

Yield: 8 servings

- Prepare Chocolate Wafer Crust, but instead of baking crust just refrigerate for 15 minutes to set crust.

- Crush chocolate toffee candy bars (a few at a time) in a food processor.

- Allow ice cream to soften; mix with chocolate toffee candy bars; place in crust and freeze.

- To make the sauce, melt butter and chocolate chips. Add the powdered sugar and milk. Stir until smooth.

- Cook about 8 minutes until thickened. Stir in vanilla.

- To serve, cut into slices and top with warm sauce. This is so rich that a small slice is best.

- Extra sauce will keep in a container in refrigerator.

## Kid Notes

» Melt butter in the microwave. Stir into the crumbs and press into the pan.

» Open candy bars and pulse to crush in a food processor, remember adult supervision!

» Stir crushed candy bar pieces into the softened ice cream. Pour into crust and put back into the freezer until firm.

# Old Fashioned Pecan Pie

*1 Homemade Pie Crust (see page 181)*
*½ cup light brown sugar*
*½ cup sugar*
*3 tablespoons flour*
*1 cup light corn syrup*
*½ teaspoon vanilla extract*
*⅛ teaspoon salt*
*3 eggs*
*¼ cup butter, melted*
*1 cup pecan halves*

## Yield: 8 servings

- Preheat oven to 300°.

- Using a 9-inch pie plate, prepare Homemade Pie Crust.

- Mix together brown sugar, sugar, and flour, use the bottom of your measuring cup like a mortar and pestle to blend the ingredients in bowl. Mix together thoroughly. Add in white corn syrup, vanilla extract, and salt, but do not mix.

- Add in eggs and stir slightly one at a time. (The more it is stirred the more likely it is to be spoiled.)

- Fold in melted butter.

- Pour mixture into unbaked pie pastry shell.

- Lay pecan halves on top of filling in circles, beginning at the outside and going in to the middle.

- Bake at 300° for 45–55 minutes or until the filling doesn't shake.

## Kid Notes

» Use measuring cup for dry ingredients to measure sugars.

» Crack the eggs into a bowl, add one at a time. (See Kid Notes on page 63.)

» Use a liquid measuring cup for the corn syrup.

» Melt the butter in the microwave (in a glass dish), about 40–50 seconds for ½ stick.

» Arrange pecan halves in a circle on top of the filling.

# Delightful Cheese Pie

### Filling:

*1 9-inch graham cracker pie crust (See page 180)*
*2 8-ounce packages of cream cheese, softened*
*2 eggs*
*1 cup sugar*
*3 teaspoons vanilla*
*Juice of one lemon (1 tablespoon)*

### Topping:

*8 ounces sour cream*
*4 tablespoons sugar*
*1 teaspoon vanilla*

Yield: 8 servings

- Preheat oven to 350°.

- Mix together cream cheese, eggs, 1 cup sugar, vanilla, and lemon juice.

- Pour into graham cracker crust.

- Bake 30–35 minutes, until the center does not shake.

- Allow to cool in refrigerator for 30 minutes.

- Put sour cream, vanilla, and sugar in a bowl and whisk.

- Spread mixture over top of cooled pie.

- Cook an additional 10 minutes at 350°.

- Allow to cool completely before cutting.

- Top with your favorite fresh fruit!

## Kid Notes

» For the lemon juice, squeeze the lemon over your hand and let your fingers catch the seeds.

» Your hand mixer works great for this recipe.

» This pie is light and easy. It tastes great with your favorite fruit on top.

# Sweetheart Fudge Pie

½ cup butter, softened
¾ cup light brown sugar, lightly packed
3 eggs
1 12-ounce package semisweet chocolate chips, melted
1 teaspoon instant coffee
1 teaspoon vanilla
½ cup all-purpose flour
1 cup walnuts or pecans, chopped
1 9-inch Cream Cheese Pie Crust (See page 179)

Yield: 8 servings

- Preheat oven to 375°.

- Cream butter and gradually add brown sugar. Beat until light and fluffy.

- Add eggs one at a time, beating well after each.

- Meanwhile, melt semisweet chocolate in a small, heavy saucepan over medium-low heat.

- Slowly pour into egg mixture and continue to mix on medium speed.

- Add instant coffee and vanilla. Mix well.

- Turn mixer on low and stir in flour and walnuts or pecans.

- Pour into unbaked pastry shell.

- Bake for 30 minutes.

## Kid Notes

» Crack the eggs into a bowl, add one at a time to the creamed mixture. (See Kids Notes on page 63.)

» Measure the flour and nuts using a dry measuring cup. Add to the mixture.

» Ask for help when pouring into a pastry shell.

# Cream Cheese Pie Crust

*1 cup all-purpose flour*
*¼ cup powdered sugar*
*Pinch salt*
*½ cup unsalted butter, cold, cubed*
*4 ounces cream cheese, cold, cubed*

**Yield: 1 pie crust, with enough extra for lattice or decorative topping**

- Blend dry ingredients in food processor fitted with a steel blade or a standing mixer with a paddle.

- Add butter and cream cheese; mix just until dough forms around blade or paddle. Wrap dough in plastic, flatten into a disk, and chill 30 minutes.

- Roll dough on lightly floured surface to 14 inches in diameter and ¼ inch thick.

- Flip and turn it often to prevent sticking.

- Fold into quarters, then unfold into a lightly greased 9-inch pie plate. Adjust dough to fit, pressing it lightly against bottom and sides of pan. Try not to stretch it or it will shrink. Trim all but 1 inch of overhand with scissors. Fold edge under and crimp.

- Freeze until firm, 15 minutes.

- Preheat oven to 400°. Line frozen shell with foil, pressing firmly against the sides and folding gently over the edges. Fill shell with raw rice or dried beans to keep the bottom from puffing up, and then "blind bake" until crust is set but not browned, about 20 minutes.

- Unfold foil at edges and carefully lift it out; return shell to oven. Bake for 5–10 minutes, or until pale golden.

- Fill as directed in recipes.

## Kid Notes

» Crimping the crust: to make an extra special crust press prongs of fork around the edge of the crust.

179

# Graham Cracker Pie Crust

*2 cups finely ground graham crackers (about 30 squares)*
*½ cup unsalted butter, melted*

**Yield: 1 pie crust**

- In a mixing bowl, combine the graham cracker crumbs and butter with a fork until evenly moistened.

- Lightly grease the bottom and sides of 9-inch pie pan.

- Pour the crumbs into the pan, and using the bottom of a measuring cup or the smooth bottom of a glass, press the crumbs down into the base and 1 inch up the sides.

- Refrigerate for 15 minutes.

# Chocolate Wafer Pie Crust

*1 18-ounce package of Oreos or chocolate wafer cookies*
*6 tablespoons butter*

**Yield: 1 pie crust**

- Preheat oven to 350°.

- Lightly grease a 9-inch pie pan.

- Crush Oreos or chocolate wafer cookies until they are fine crumbs. This can be done in the food processor.

- Melt butter.

- Mix with Oreos or chocolate wafer cookies.

- Pour the crumbs into the pan, and using the bottom of a measuring cup or the smooth bottom of a glass, press the crumbs down into the base and 1 inch up the sides.

- Bake pie crust for 10 minutes.

## Kid Notes

» Place graham crackers in food processor and pulse until fine, remember to ask your adult helper for assistance.

» Place butter in glass bowl and microwave about 50 seconds until melted.

» Mix together and press into pie plate.

## Kid Notes

» Place chocolate wafers in food processor and pulse fine.

» Place butter in glass bowl and microwave for about 50 seconds until melted.

» Combine ingredients and press into pie plate.

# Homemade Pie Crust

*2 cups all-purpose flour*
*1 teaspoon salt*
*¼ cup cold water*
*⅔ cup chilled shortening (for buttery flavor crust use*
*butter-flavored shortening)*

**Yield: 1 pie crust**

- Add salt to flour.

- In large bowl, mix flour and shortening with pastry blender or work lightly with tips of fingers. Do this until crumbly.

- Add cold water slowly to the bowl of dough and mix well.

- Gather dough into large ball. Handle lightly to incorporate as much air as possible. This will make a flaky crust.

- Lightly flour a work surface and roll dough to a 14-inch round, about 1/8-inch thick. (If using a pastry cloth, less flour is needed on work surface.)

- Dust rolling pin and dough with flour as needed. (If dough has been refrigerated, bring to room temperature.) Roll from the center out. Roll continuously in the same direction, lifting your rolling pin and moving back to the center to roll again.

- Fold into quarters, then unfold into a lightly greased 9-inch pie plate. Press lightly against bottom and sides of dish. Trim all but 1 inch of overhang with scissors, fold edge under, and crimp.

- If your crust tears, patch together gently with your fingers using excess dough from another part of the crust—do not reroll.

## Kid Notes

» Work the shortening into the flour by using a pastry blender, two table knives, or your fingers. This tenderizes the pastry.

» The dough should form a ball that is firm and not too wet.

» Remember to press down on the dough with the rolling pin and roll out to the North, South, East, and West.

» Too much shortening makes the crust greasy.

» Too much flour makes it tough.

» Too much water makes it soggy.

# bake sale favorites

When we were little girls, a popular television commercial of the day claimed "Nothing says lovin' like something from the oven." This simple saying cleverly expressed a universal truth that nothing warms the heart and fills the home like the aroma of baking. The recipes in this chapter are family recipes that were cooked with love in our grandmothers' and mothers' kitchens. We just couldn't write a cookbook without including them. Our grandmothers, Annette Shepherd of New Orleans and Helen Todd of Hattiesburg, Mississippi, and our mothers, Mary Lynn Andrews and Dorothy Puckett, believed that children should not only be seen and heard, but welcome in the family kitchen. Just as they were handed down to us, we pass these recipes along to you in hopes that they will create magical food memories for your family as they did for ours.

Granny's Cheese Straws
Leslie's Fluffy Ladies
Conglomerations
La-Te-Dahs!
Rob's Ranger Cookies
Helen's Peanut Butter M&M
  Cookies
Gingersnaps
Glazed Sugar Cookies

Mrs. Todd's Cream Cheese
  Pound Cake
Grandmother's No-Fail
  Pumpkin Bread
Royal Carrot Cake
Tunnel of Fudge Cake
Poppy Seed Bread
So Good Banana Bread
Sterling's Simply Spectacular
  Brownies
Kim's Raspberry Bars

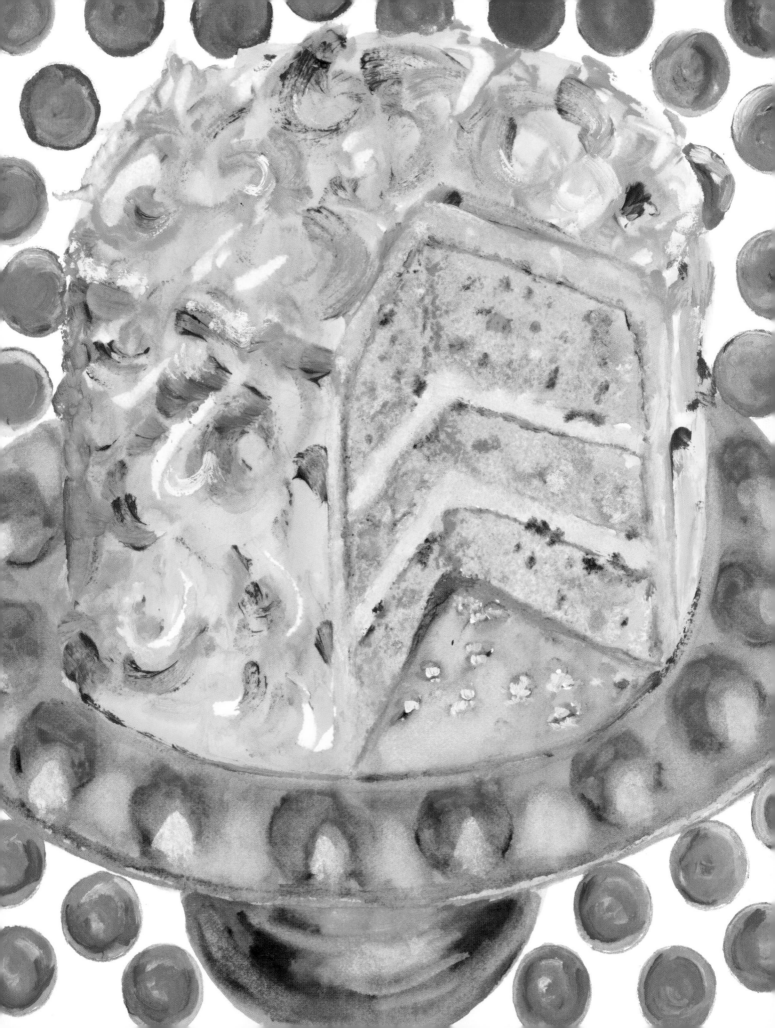

# Granny's Cheese Straws

*1 cup margarine, room temperature*
*12 ounces extra sharp cheddar cheese, grated*
*2 cups flour*
*⅛ teaspoon salt*
*½ teaspoon cayenne or red pepper*

### Yield: 4–5 dozen

- Preheat oven to 350°.

- Cream margarine and cheese in mixer on medium-high speed for 5 minutes until very creamy.

- Sift flour, salt, and cayenne and gradually add to the creamed mixture.

- Place dough in a cookie press and make long strips on a cookie sheet.

- Bake for 8–10 minutes.

- Remove from oven.

- With a table knife, cut into 3–4-inch "straws."

- When cool, remove from pan with a spatula. Store in an airtight container.

## Kid Notes

» You can use a hand mixer or a standing mixer—the butter and cheese need to be very creamy before adding the flour.

» Sift the dry ingredients together.

» Once you get the hang of using a cookie press, there is nothing to it!

» These cheese straws go fast! They are nice to give as a gift and are welcomed at any gathering.

## Kid Notes

» Wax paper works great when pressing the dough into the pan.

» Use the tips or your finger and spread dough all over the baking dish.

» The pecans can be chopped in a food processor by pushing the pulse button on and off until coarsely chopped.

» Your job is to unwrap all the caramels!

# Leslie's Fluffy Ladies

*1 roll refrigerated chocolate chip cookie dough*
*6 ounces semisweet chocolate chips*
*1 12-ounce bag caramels*
*3 tablespoons half and half*
*1 cup pecans, chopped*

## Yield: 24 2-inch squares

- Preheat oven to 350°.

- Grease a 9- by 13-inch baking dish.

- Press cookie dough into baking dish and bake according to dough directions.

- Sprinkle with chocolate chips and bake for about 5 minutes more.

- Meanwhile, unwrap caramels and put in a pan; add half and half.

- Stir caramels and half and half over medium heat until caramels are melted.

- Pour over chocolate chips and spread evenly.

- Sprinkle with chopped pecans.

- Put in refrigerator to cool.

- Cut into bars when completely cool.

# Conglomerations

*1 cup butter, melted*
*1 pound confectioners' sugar*
*1½ cups crunchy or creamy peanut butter*
*12 graham crackers*
*6  1.55-ounce Hershey milk chocolate bars*

**Yield: 24 2-inch squares**

- Preheat oven to 400°.

- Line a 9- by 13-inch pan with aluminum foil.

- Place the graham crackers side by side on the foil.

- Melt the butter in a saucepan.

- Stir in the peanut butter and confectioners' sugar. Remove from stove top.

- Spread the peanut butter mixture over the graham crackers.

- Break the milk chocolate bars into pieces and lay them over the peanut butter mixture.

- Bake for 5–7 minutes until chocolate softens.

- Remove from oven and spread chocolate all over.

- Place in refrigerator to cool before cutting.

- The conglomerations will keep at room temperature until they are all gone—not very long!

Note: Chocolate and cinnamon graham crackers work just as well as the original graham crackers.

## Kid Notes

» Line the pan with aluminum foil. Place the graham crackers on top, putting them side by side with no space in between.

» The peanut butter mixture is thick but spreadable.

» Open the Hershey bars, break into pieces, and spread over top of peanut butter mixture.

» Ask for help when placing in and removing from the oven.

# La-Te-Dahs!

*2 cups unsalted butter*
*1 cup dark brown sugar, packed*
*1 cup light brown sugar, packed*
*3 large eggs, beaten*
*1 tablespoon vanilla*
*2 tablespoons cinnamon*
*½ teaspoon ginger*
*2 cups sugar*
*2 cups flour*
*2 teaspoons salt*
*2 teaspoons baking soda*
*3 cups quick-cooking oatmeal*
*2 cups walnut pieces*
*1 cup raisins*

**Yield: 24 2-inch squares**

- Preheat oven to 350°.

- Line cookie sheets with parchment paper.

- Cream together butter and brown sugars until light and fluffy.

- Add beaten eggs and vanilla.

- Combine cinnamon, ginger, and white sugar, and add slowly to creamed mixture.

- Sift together flour, salt, and baking soda, and slowly add to sugar mixture.

- Blend in oatmeal; then stir in walnut pieces and raisins.

- Drop by rounded tablespoons onto cookie sheets, about 2 inches apart.

- Bake 9–11 minutes.

- Remove cookie sheets from oven, bang sharply on counter. Remove cookies with a spatula and place cookies on brown paper bag to cool. (This step is very important!)

## Kid Notes

» When you measure brown sugar, you must "pack" according to the directions. When the recipe calls for "Packed," you press the brown sugar into the cup to the desired measuring line. "Lightly packed" means to scoop the sugar into the measuring cup to the desired measuring line with no pressing or packing it in. Of course, there is less sugar in a "lightly packed" measure.

» Use a standing mixer or hand mixer and cream butter and sugar until light and fluffy.

# Rob's Ranger Cookies

*1 cup butter-flavored shortening*
*1 cup sugar*
*1 cup light brown sugar, lightly packed*
*2 eggs*
*1 teaspoon vanilla*
*2 cups all-purpose flour*
*1 teaspoon baking soda*
*1 teaspoon baking powder*
*½ teaspoon salt*
*2 cups quick-cooking oatmeal*
*2 cups Rice Krispies*

## Yield: 6 dozen

- Preheat oven to 350°.

- Grease cookie sheet or line with parchment paper.

- Cream the shortening and sugars together.

- Add the eggs and vanilla; mix until smooth.

- Sift flour, baking powder, baking soda, and salt together; add to creamed mixture. Mix well.

- Add the oatmeal and rice cereal and mix.

- For each cookie, drop a heaping tablespoon of cookie dough onto cookie sheet about ½ inch apart and press slightly.

- Bake at 350° for 8–10 minutes.

## Kid Notes

» Cream the shortening and sugar for about 4–5 minutes until really creamy.

» Crack the eggs in a separate bowl and add. (See Kid Notes on page 63.)

» Measure the dry ingredients and sift together.

» Measure the oatmeal and Rice Krispies—add last.

## Kid Notes

» A dry measuring cup is one that you do not pour out of.

» Sift the dry ingredients together.

» Crack the eggs (see Kid notes page 63).

» Cream butter, peanut butter, and sugar using a hand mixer or a standing mixer.

» You can make giant cookies by putting two tablespoons of dough together on the baking sheet.

» Ask for help when placing the pan in and removing it from the oven.

# Helen's Peanut Butter M&M Cookies

2 cups flour
1 teaspoon baking soda
1 teaspoon salt
¼ teaspoon cinnamon
¾ cup unsalted butter, softened
¾ cup peanut butter
1 cup sugar
1 cup light brown sugar, lightly packed
2 eggs
1 teaspoon vanilla extract
¼ cup milk
2 cups old fashioned oatmeal (not quick cooking)
12-ounce bag of M&M baking chips

**Yield: 2 dozen**

- Preheat oven to 325°.

- Lightly grease a baking sheet or line with parchment paper.

- Sift the flour, salt, baking soda, and cinnamon. Set aside.

- In a large bowl cream butter, peanut butter, and sugars.

- Beat in the eggs one by one. Add vanilla.

- Add the milk and the flour mixture. Beat until well blended.

- Stir in the oatmeal and chocolate chips.

- Drop by rounded tablespoons onto baking sheet, about 2 inches apart.

- Bake for 10–12 minutes.

- Let sit for a minute before moving to a cooling rack.

# Gingersnaps

¾ cup butter, softened
1 cup sugar
¼ cup molasses
¼ teaspoon salt
1 teaspoon cinnamon
2 teaspoons baking soda
1 teaspoon cloves
1 teaspoon ginger
2 cups all-purpose flour, sifted
sugar for rolling cookies

### Yield: About 2 dozen

- Preheat oven to 350°.

- Lightly grease a baking sheet or line with parchment.

- Cream together butter and sugar. Add molasses and mix thoroughly.

- Add salt, cinnamon, baking soda, cloves, and ginger; mix well.

- Sift flour and add to the mix. Form dough into 1-inch balls and roll in sugar. Place on baking sheet about 2 inches apart.

- Bake for 10–12 minutes.

## Kid Notes

» To soften butter, put it in your mixing bowl about an hour (or more) before you begin to make the cookies.

» Measure the molasses in a liquid measuring cup.

» Use measuring spoons for the salt, cinnamon, baking soda, cloves, and ginger.

» Sift the flour and add.

» Roll the dough into balls and roll the balls in sugar that is in a shallow bowl. (Start with about ½ cup and add more if you need to.)

» Ask for help when placing the pan in and removing from the oven.

## Kid Notes

» Cream butter by using a hand mixer or a standing mixer.

» Measure sugar in a dry measuring cup and add slowly to the butter.

» Measure cream of tartar, baking soda, and salt using measuring spoons. Add to creamed mixture.

» Crack 1 egg into a bowl. If it is good, add it to the mixture and beat. Repeat with the second egg (see Kid Notes on page 63).

» Measure the vanilla with a measuring spoon and add.

» The reason for refrigerating the dough is so that it will be easier to roll into balls.

» For the glaze, stir all ingredients together using a whisk. Pick out your favorite food color and tint the icing. Or you can use several colors by dividing the icing into different bowls and tinting separately.

# Glazed Sugar Cookies

1 cup butter, softened
1½ cups sugar
2 teaspoons cream of tartar
1 teaspoon baking soda
¼ teaspoon salt
2 eggs
1 teaspoon vanilla extract
2½ cups all-purpose flour

**Glaze:**
3–4 teaspoons milk
1 teaspoon vanilla extract
½ teaspoon almond extract
Assorted food color
1 cup confectioners' sugar
Sprinkles, optional

**Yield: About 3 dozen**

- Preheat oven to 375°. In a large bowl, cream butter for 30 seconds. Blend in sugar, cream of tartar, baking soda, and salt. Beat in eggs and 1 teaspoon vanilla extract. Mix in as much of the flour as possible with mixer. Use a wooden spoon to stir in any remaining flour.

- Cover and chill 1 hour or until dough is firm. Shape dough into 1-inch balls and place 2 inches apart on ungreased cookie sheet.

- Bake 8-10 minutes, or until edges are lightly brown. Let cool and decorate with colored glaze as desired.

## Glaze

- Combine milk and 1 teaspoon vanilla extract; stir in confectioners' sugar. Add a bit more milk to thin or more confectioners' sugar to stiffen. Blend in 3–4 drops food color, or if desired, divide the icing among separate small bowls and tint each a different color with 1–2 drops of food color.

- Use a spoon to pour and spread over the cookies. Add sprinkles if desired.

# Mrs. Todd's Cream Cheese Pound Cake

*3 cups sugar*
*1½ cups butter, softened*
*8 ounces cream cheese, softened*
*3 cups all-purpose flour, sifted*
*½ teaspoon salt*
*6 eggs*
*1 tablespoon lemon flavoring (extract)*
*1 tablespoon almond flavoring (extract)*

**Yield: 10–12 servings**

- Preheat oven to 325°.

- Grease and flour 10-inch tube pan or bundt cake pan.

- In a large bowl cream sugar, butter, and cream cheese until light and fluffy.

- Sift flour and salt together.

- Alternately add eggs and flour to the creamed mixture, beginning and ending with flour.

- Add flavorings.

- Beat until smooth and blended.

- Bake for 1 hour and 15 minutes.

- Cool before removing from pan.

## Kid Notes

» Place the cream cheese and butter into your mixing bowl about an hour before you begin.

» Crack the eggs into a bowl and add one at a time, beating in about ½ cup of the sifted flour mixture in after each (see Kid Notes on page 63).

» Ask for help when placing in and removing from the oven.

## Grandmother's No-Fail Pumpkin Bread

*3 cups sugar*
*1 cup canola or vegetable oil*
*3 eggs*
*2 cups canned pumpkin*
*3 cups all-purpose flour, sifted*
*½ teaspoon baking soda*
*1 teaspoon salt*
*1 teaspoon cinnamon*
*1 teaspoon nutmeg*

**Yield: 2 large loaves**

- Preheat oven to 325°.

- Grease two 9- by 5- by 3-inch loaf pans

- Sift together dry ingredients and set aside.

- In a large mixing bowl, add sugar and oil and blend. Add eggs one at a time and beat well, using a whisk.

- Mix pumpkin into egg mixture.

- Add sifted dry ingredients and mix thoroughly.

- Pour batter into loaf pans and let stand for 20 minutes.

- Bake at 325° for an hour and a half, or until done.

### Kid Notes

» Crack the egg (see Kid Notes on page 63).

» Measure oil in a liquid measuring cup.

» Grease loaf pans and pour batter evenly into each.

» Ask for help when placing in and removing from the oven.

# Royal Carrot Cake

### Pecan Cream Filling:

1½ cups sugar
¼ cup flour
¾ teaspoon salt
1½ cups heavy cream
¾ cup butter
1¼ cups pecans, chopped
2 teaspoons vanilla extract

### Carrot Cake:

1¼ cups corn oil
2 cups sugar
2 cups all-purpose flour
2 teaspoons cinnamon
2 teaspoons baking powder
1 teaspoon baking soda
1 teaspoon salt
4 eggs
4 cups carrots, grated (about a 1-pound bag)
1 cup pecans, chopped
1 cup raisins

### Cream Cheese Frosting:

8 ounces butter, softened
8 ounces cream cheese, softened
1 1-pound box powdered sugar
1 tablespoon vanilla extract

### Assembly:

1½ cups sweetened shredded coconut

Yield: 12 servings

### Pecan Cream Filling:

- Combine the sugar, flour, and salt in a heavy saucepan. Slowly whisk in the cream. Add the butter.

- Over low heat, cook and stir the mixture until the butter melts. Continue to cook for 20 minutes, stirring occasionally. Filling should be brown in color.

- Cool for 15 minutes.

- Stir in the nuts and vanilla extract.

- Allow to cool completely and then refrigerate, preferably overnight.

- If the mixture is too thick to spread when ready to use, bring it to room temperature.

### Carrot Cake:

- Preheat oven to 350°.

- Grease and flour 10-inch tube cake pan.

- In a large bowl, whisk the corn oil and sugar together.

- In a separate bowl, sift the flour, cinnamon, baking powder, baking soda, and salt together.
- Blend half of the sifted ingredients into the sugar-oil mixture.
- Add eggs, one by one, alternating with dry ingredients. Combine well using a whisk.
- Add the grated carrots, raisins, and pecans.
- Pour into the greased tube pan and bake for 1 hour and 10 minutes.
- Cool upright in the pan on a cooling rack.

## Cream Cheese Frosting:

- Cream the butter until light and fluffy.
- Add the cream cheese and beat until well blended.
- Sift the powdered sugar and add to the butter mixture. Mix until well blended.
- Add vanilla extract and mix well.

### Kid Notes

» This cake has several parts. Don't worry though. Just make the three recipes and put them together to make one outstanding cake!

» Crack eggs (see Kid Notes on page 63).

» Measure and sift dry ingredients.

» Ask for assistance when cooking on stove top and placing cake in the oven and taking out of oven.

- Refrigerate if not using immediately, but bring to a spreadable temperature before using.

## Assembly:

- Preheat the oven to 300°.
- Spread the coconut on a baking sheet and bake for 10–15 minutes, stirring occasionally, until it lightly colors. Cool.
- Have the filling and frosting at a spreadable consistency.
- Loosen the cake in its pan and invert onto a serving plate.
- Carefully split the cake into 3 horizontal layers using a long serrated knife.
- Spread the filling between the layers.
- Spread the frosting over the top and sides.
- Pat the toasted coconut onto the sides of the cake.

# Tunnel of Fudge Cake

## Cake:

1¾ cups butter, softened
1¾ cups sugar
6 eggs
2 cups powdered sugar
2¼ cups all-purpose flour
¾ cup cocoa
2 cups walnuts, chopped

## Glaze:

¾ cup powdered sugar
¼ cup cocoa
3½–4 tablespoons milk

Yield: 16 servings

- Preheat oven to 350°.

- Grease and flour a bundt cake pan.

- In a large bowl, beat butter and sugar until light and fluffy. Add eggs, one at a time, beating well after each one.

- Gradually add powdered sugar; blend well. By hand, stir in remaining cake ingredients until well blended.

- Spoon batter into prepared pan; spread evenly.

- Bake for 58–60 minutes.* Cool upright in pan on cooling rack 1 hour; invert onto serving plate. Cool completely.

- In small bowl, combine glaze ingredients until well blended. Spoon over top of cake, allowing some to run down sides.

- Store tightly covered.

*Since this cake has a soft tunnel of fudge, ordinary doneness test cannot be used. Accurate oven temperature and bake time are critical.

Tip—Nuts are essential for the success of the recipe.

## Kid Notes

» Crack eggs (see Kid Notes on page 63).

» Measure and sift dry ingredients.

» Beat butter and sugar until creamy using a hand or standing mixer.

» Combine glaze ingredients while cake is cooling.

## Kid Notes

» Measure the oil using a liquid measuring cup.

» Crack the eggs one at a time in a bowl, and if they are good add them to the batter (see Kid Notes on page 63).

» Sift the dry ingredients.

» Pour the batter into the loaf pans.

» Ask for help when placing the pans in and removing them from the oven.

# Poppy Seed Bread

*2 cups sugar*
*1¼ cup oil*
*4 eggs*
*1 12-ounce can evaporated milk*
*4 cups all-purpose flour*
*4 teaspoons baking powder*
*1 teaspoon salt*
*1 teaspoon vanilla*
*½ cup poppy seeds*

**Yield: 2 large loaves**

- Preheat oven to 325°.

- Grease 2 large loaf pans.

- Beat sugar and oil on medium speed until thoroughly blended.

- Add eggs one at a time beating after each.

- Sift together dry ingredients. Slowly add dry ingredients to the sugar mixture.

- Add evaporated milk and blend.

- Stir in vanilla and poppy seeds.

- Pour batter into loaf pans.

- Bake for 35 minutes, or until lightly browned.

# So Good Banana Bread

½ cup shortening
½ cup butter
2 cups sugar
1 cup light brown sugar, lightly packed
2 teaspoons vanilla
4 eggs
½ teaspoon salt
3½ cups all-purpose flour
2 teaspoons baking soda
½ cup buttermilk
6 small bananas, mashed
1 cup pecans, chopped (optional)

**Yield: 2 loaves**

- Preheat oven to 350°.

- Grease 2 loaf pans.

- In a large bowl, cream shortening, butter, sugar, and vanilla until fluffy.

- Add eggs one at a time, blending thoroughly after each addition.

- In a separate bowl, sift salt, flour, and baking soda twice.

- Add dry ingredients alternately with milk to the creamy mixture.

- Combine bananas and nuts and blend into mixture.

- Pour into a greased loaf pans and cook in 350° oven for 55–60 minutes.

## Kid Notes

» Crack eggs (see Kid Notes page 63).

» Sift and measure dry ingredients.

» Beat butter and sugars until very creamy using a hand or standing mixer.

» Alternate adding dry ingredients with the buttermilk and baking soda mixture.

» Peel and mash bananas. (Brownish bananas work best!) Add to mixture.

» Grease loaf pans and divide batter filling ⅔ full.

## Kid Notes

» This is the most wonderful old-fashioned brownie recipe you will ever own.

» Ask for assistance when cooking on the stove top.

» Double sift means sift twice!

» Crack eggs (see Kid Notes page 63).

» A spatula is the best tool to take the brownies out of the pan.

# Sterling's Simply Spectacular Brownies

1 cup butter
2½ cups sugar
2 squares unsweetened baking chocolate
1 square semisweet baking chocolate
2 pinches salt
1½ cups all-purpose flour
½ teaspoon baking powder
4 eggs
2 teaspoons vanilla extract

**Yield: 32 brownies**

- Preheat oven to 300°.

- Lightly grease two 8-inch square brownie pans. (If you use one large pan, the batter will thin out too much.)

- Melt butter, sugar, and chocolate in medium-sized (2-quart) saucepan on top of stove. Stir well with a spatula with a square front as this is flexible and will not let anything accrue at the bottom of the pan. (You can use a wooden spoon if you do not have a heat-tolerant spatula.) Remove from heat.

- Double-sift flour, add baking powder, and set aside.

- Break eggs into saucepan of chocolate when it has cooled a little. (You may want to break into a bowl first, just in case you get any shells.)

- Stir well; use hand mixer if necessary.

- Add vanilla extract and salt to chocolate in saucepan. Stir well.

- Add double-sifted flour to chocolate in saucepan. Stir well.

- Split the chocolate mixture evenly between the two brownie pans.

- Cook for 40 minutes. Remove immediately, even if they do not seem done.

- Let sit in pan for 5–8 minutes, no longer or they will overcook.

- Cut into 16 brownies per brownie pan. Be careful because they will still be hot.

# Kim's Raspberry Bars

## Crust:
1¼ cups all-purpose flour
⅓ cup light brown sugar, lightly packed
½ cup (1 stick) butter, cold and cut into 8 pieces
1¼ cup raspberry preserves, seedless, or apricot
   preserves

## Topping:
¾ cup all-purpose flour
1½ cups light brown sugar, lightly packed
¼ cup (½ stick) butter, cold and cut into 4 pieces
⅛ teaspoon salt
1 teaspoon almond extract

## Icing:
1 cup powdered sugar
1 tablespoon milk

Yield: 24 2-inch squares

### Kid Notes
» These taste like homemade pop tarts!

» Put the butter, flour, and sugar in the food processor and pulse only until blended.

» Ask for help when placing the pan in and removing it from the oven.

» While it is cooking the second time, combine the glaze ingredients. Drizzle over top when cool.

## Crust:

- Preheat oven to 350°. Grease a jelly roll pan.

- Put flour, brown sugar, and butter pieces into a food processor. Pulse until the butter is completely mixed into the flour and sugar. Pat evenly into a jelly roll pan.

- Bake for 10 minutes. Remove from oven and cool.

## Topping:

- Place the ingredients in the food processor and pulse until completely combined.

- Spread the raspberry (or apricot) preserves thinly all across the cooled crust.

- Sprinkle the topping all over the preserves.

- Bake for 12 to 15 minutes. Cool.

## Icing:

- Combine icing ingredients and stir until blended. Drizzle over cooled bars.

- Cut into squares and enjoy!

# Kitchen Notes

# afterword

Leslie Carpenter and Helen DeFrance wrote the book on teaching kids to cook. *At Home Café: Great Food and Fun for Everyone!* serves up cooking as a family activity where the kids are full participants in the meal-making process.

The former caterers met while both were teaching cooking classes at The Everyday Gourmet, a Jackson, Mississippi, cooking school, and discovered an immediate rapport. Soon they were teaching month-long children's courses together and developing a joint venture known as Kids Are Cooking! with Helen and Leslie. Kids Are Cooking! with Helen and Leslie now offers classes at preschools, schools, cooking schools, and luxury hotels such as the prestigious Blackberry Farm near Knoxville, Tennessee.

Leslie and Helen prefer a hands-on approach to teaching kids to cook, involving them in every aspect of meal preparation from menu planning to grocery shopping, cooking, eating the delicious results, and cleaning up. With the publication of *At Home Café*, Helen and Leslie are taking their message of bringing families together through cooking on the road and into homes all across America.

Learn more about Leslie and Helen and their Kids Are Cooking! with Helen and Leslie programs at www.athomecafe.net.

Leslie Andrews Carpenter is a native of Greenville, Mississippi. She attributes her love of cooking to her New Orleans-born parents and their heritage of communal cooking and eating. Leslie holds a degree in education from the University of Mississippi, where she was awarded the title of Miss Ole Miss. Leslie lives in Jackson with her husband, Phillip, and their four children Rob, William, Myers, and Annie.

Helen Puckett DeFrance was born and raised in Jackson, Mississippi. The fourth child in a family of six children, she learned cooking from her grandmother, Helen Todd. She holds a masters degree in education from Pepperdine University with an emphasis in the Montessori method of education, which promotes a "hands-on" approach to learning. Helen and her son, Martin, live in Jackson.

Dea Dea Adams Baker is a Jackson, Mississippi, artist who finds inspiration in the world around her—whether a bag of groceries or the landscape of the Tuscan countryside. Her joyful spirit and colorful personality are reflected in her watercolors that appear in galleries across the country. Dea Dea is wife to Dolph and mother to Rachel and Jessi.

Carol Puckett Daily, creative writer for this book, is the founder of The Everyday Gourmet, a Jackson, Mississippi-based cooking store. She serves as Director of Special Projects for Viking Range Corporation where her current "special projects" are the new Viking Cooking School and the Alluvian Hotel in Greenwood, Mississippi.

# index